Fondant Modeling
for Cake Decorators

Fondant Modeling for Cake Decorators

Helen
Penman

FIREFLY BOOKS

contents

A FIREFLY BOOK

Published by Firefly Books Ltd. 2011

Copyright © 2011 Quarto Inc.

First printing

Publisher Cataloging-in-Publication Data (U.S.)
Penman, Helen.
   Fondant modeling for cake decorators : 100 fondant features to top off a special cake /
Helen Penman.
[256] p. : col. photos. ; cm.
Includes index.
Summary: The essential techniques, materials, and recipes for all the essential elements of a fondant cake.
ISBN-13: 978-1-55407-913-1
1. Fondant. 2. Cake decorating.
3. Cake. I. Title.
641.8653 dc22   TX771.2. 2011

Library and Archives Canada Cataloguing in Publication
Penman, Helen
   Fondant modeling for cake decorators : 100 fondant features to top off a special cake / Helen Penman.
Includes index.
ISBN 978-1-55407-913-1
1. Cake decorating. 2. Fondant.
I. Title.
TX771.2.P46 2011
641.8′6539   C2011-903451-4

Published in the United States by
Firefly Books (U.S.) Inc.
P.O. Box 1338, Ellicott Station
Buffalo, New York 14205

Published in Canada by
Firefly Books Ltd.
66 Leek Crescent
Richmond Hill, Ontario L4B 1H1

Conceived, designed, and
produced by
Quarto Publishing plc
The Old Brewery
6 Blundell Street
London N7 9BH

Senior editor: Chloe Todd Fordham
Art editor: Joanna Bettles
Designer: Susi Martin
Design assistant:
Alison Van Kerkhoff
Picture researcher:
Sarah Bell
Photographer:
Philip Wilkins
Illustrator: Coral Mula,
Kuo Kang Chen
U.S. cake consultant: Phyllis Lester
Art director: Caroline Guest
Creative director: Moira Clinch
Publisher: Paul Carslake

Color separation in China by Modern
Age Pte Ltd
Printed in Hong Kong by Midas
Printing International, Ltd

about this book

Fondant cake toppers are an attractive and fun part of cake decorating. This books shows you how to make over 100 different toppers suitable for birthday cakes, wedding cakes and more. The book is organized as follows.

Topper Selector (pages 8–17)

Looking for inspiration? Browse the topper selector on pages 8–17, choose your favorite design, turn to the page listed, and follow the basic instructions to create your fondant model.

Tools, Recipes and Techniques (pages 18–85)

Up front you will learn how to bake and prepare the perfect cake to show off your topper, as well as information on tools and equipment and essential techniques such as piping, leveling and working with paste.

Materials and tools
These lists ensure you have all the right equipment at hand.

Charts and tables
Measurements are given in imperial and metric. Choose one or the other; do not mix the two.

Step-by-step photos
Full-color photography takes you step-by-step through the core techniques of cake baking and cake decorating.

TERMINOLOGY
For an at-a-glance guide to the cake decorating terminology used in this book, turn to page 255.

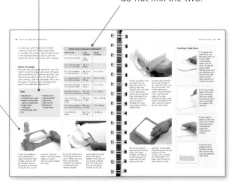

Topper Directory (pages 86–249)

Starting on page 86 is the Topper Directory, a comprehensive library of topper designs, which takes you step-by-step through the basic formation of cake toppers by building on the techniques learned in the previous chapter. Toppers are organized by theme as follows: creative creatures (pages 88–115), flowers and fruit (pages 116–131), celebrations (pages 132–197), passions (pages 198–225), and fantasy (pages 226–249).

Deconstructed model
Each model is uniquely presented in an "exploded" format, revealing individual components and how they fit together.

Completed topper
Full-color photography illustrates the finished cake topper.

Materials and tools
Here you will find listed all the tools and fondant colors required to make the model.

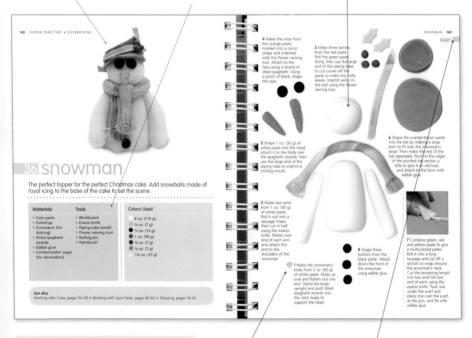

142 | TOPPER DIRECTORY • CELEBRATIONS

SNOWMAN | 143

EASY

4 Make the nose from the orange paste, molded into a carrot shape and indented with the flower veining tool. Attach to the face using a strand of dried spaghetti. Using a pinch of black, shape the eyes.

5 Make three berries from the red paste. Roll the green paste thinly, then use the large end of the piping tube to cut curves off the paste to make tiny holly leaves. Imprint veins on the leaf using the flower veining tool.

6 Shape the orange-brown paste into the hat by making a large brim to fit over the snowman's head. Then make the rest of the hat separately. Pinch in the edges of the pointed hat section a little to give it an old look, and attach to the brim with edible glue.

3 Shape 1 oz. (30 g) of white paste into the head, attach it to the body over the spaghetti strands, then use the large end of the piping tube to imprint a smiling mouth.

36 snowman

The perfect topper for the perfect Christmas cake. Add snowballs made of royal icing to the base of the cake to set the scene.

2 Make two arms from 1 oz. (30 g) of white paste Roll it out into a sausage shape, then cut in half using the exacto knife. Flatten one end of each arm and attach this end to the shoulders of the snowman.

7 Combine green, red and yellow paste to give a multicolored paste. Roll it into a long sausage and cut off a section to wrap around the snowman's neck. Cut the remaining length into two and frill one end of each using the exacto knife. Tuck one under the scarf and place one over the scarf, at the join, and fix with edible glue.

8 Shape three buttons from the black paste. Attach down the front of the snowman using edible glue.

1 Make the snowman's body from 2 oz. (60 g) of white paste. Make an oval and flatten out one end. Stand the body upright and push dried spaghetti strands into the neck ready to support the head.

Materials	Tools	Colors Used	
• Gum paste	• Workboard		4 oz. (115 g)
• Colorings	• Exacto knife		¼ oz. (7 g)
• Cornstarch (for dusting)	• Piping tube (small)		½ oz. (15 g)
• Dried spaghetti strands	• Flower veining tool		1 oz. (30 g)
• Edible glue	• Rolling pin		¼ oz. (7 g)
• Confectioners' sugar (for decoration)	• Paintbrush		¼ oz. (7 g)
			1¼ oz. (37 g)

See also
Working with Color, pages 54–59 > Working with Gum Paste, pages 60–63 > Texturing, pages 74–81

WARNING
Wire is a choking hazard. If you use wire in your toppers, remember to tell the recipient that you have done so. Avoid using wire in toppers intended for small children.

"Start here" icon
The first step in the sequence is indicated by this orange icon. Start here and work clockwise.

Skill level
Skill level (easy, intermediate, advanced) is indicated here. Start with an easy model and move up when you feel comfortable.

topper selector

Choose your favorite design, turn to the page listed, and follow the basic instructions to create your fondant model.

Lion 1

Crocodile 2

Elephant 3

Dinosaur 4

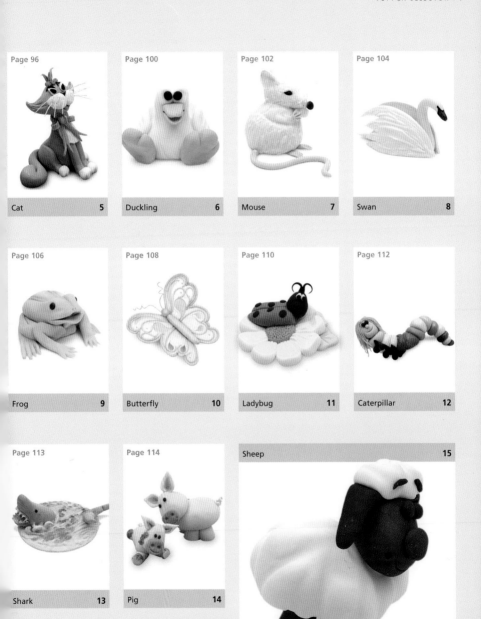

Wedding Bells 60

Bows 61

Bows 62

Bows 63

Bows 64

New Baby 65

New Baby 66

New Baby 67

New Baby 68

Rag Doll 69

Clown 70

tools, recipes and techniques

In these pages are all the essential techniques and materials you need to get started making your fondant models—plus recipes for cakes, frostings and fondants.

tools and equipment

The cake toppers within these pages are made using various sugarcraft tools; however, it is not necessary for you to buy them all. Instead, start with the beginner's tools (starred [✪] items below). Then, add to your supplies as you become more proficient and are ready to tackle more challenging toppers. Basic baking equipment is also required, and some kitchen tools are ideal for topper making, as well as for making the cake.

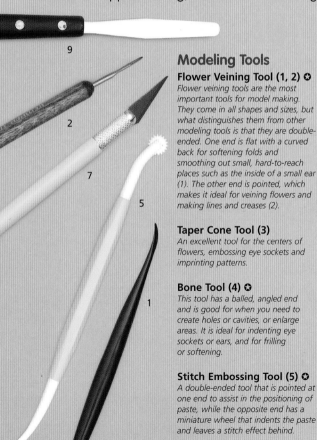

Modeling Tools

Flower Veining Tool (1, 2) ✪
Flower veining tools are the most important tools for model making. They come in all shapes and sizes, but what distinguishes them from other modeling tools is that they are double-ended. One end is flat with a curved back for softening folds and smoothing out small, hard-to-reach places such as the inside of a small ear (1). The other end is pointed, which makes it ideal for veining flowers and making lines and creases (2).

Taper Cone Tool (3)
An excellent tool for the centers of flowers, embossing eye sockets and imprinting patterns.

Bone Tool (4) ✪
This tool has a balled, angled end and is good for when you need to create holes or cavities, or enlarge areas. It is ideal for indenting eye sockets or ears, and for frilling or softening.

Stitch Embossing Tool (5) ✪
A double-ended tool that is pointed at one end to assist in the positioning of paste, while the opposite end has a miniature wheel that indents the paste and leaves a stitch effect behind.

Ball and Scallop Tool (6)
The ball end is perfect for smoothing indentations and the scalloped end creates a delightful embossed design on paste.

Sugarcraft Scalpel (7) ✪
This exacto knife is a useful tool when you need to cut small pieces out neatly and accurately. It is also excellent for neatening paste in inaccessible areas.

Pizza Wheel (8)
A perfect tool to use when slicing and cutting long, smooth sections of paste. It is also useful when cutting freehand pieces that vary in width.

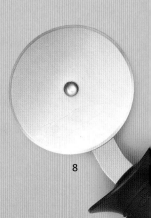

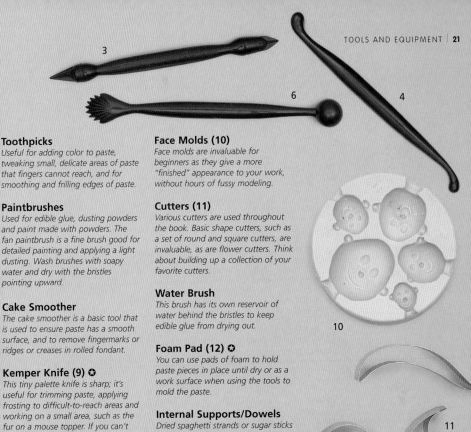

Toothpicks
Useful for adding color to paste, tweaking small, delicate areas of paste that fingers cannot reach, and for smoothing and frilling edges of paste.

Paintbrushes
Used for edible glue, dusting powders and paint made with powders. The fan paintbrush is a fine brush good for detailed painting and applying a light dusting. Wash brushes with soapy water and dry with the bristles pointing upward.

Cake Smoother
The cake smoother is a basic tool that is used to ensure paste has a smooth surface, and to remove fingermarks or ridges or creases in rolled fondant.

Kemper Knife (9) ✪
This tiny palette knife is sharp; it's useful for trimming paste, applying frosting to difficult-to-reach areas and working on a small area, such as the fur on a mouse topper. If you can't find a Kemper knife, use a small palette knife.

Ribbon Cutter
A ribbon cutter can be altered to any width and will accurately cut out a ribbon of paste.

Workboard
An acrylic surface is ideal for rolling and working on fondant pastes.

Rolling Pin
An acrylic rolling pin is best as it is heavier and rolls paste smoothly. If you can't find an acrylic rolling pin, a household wooden one will do.

Face Molds (10)
Face molds are invaluable for beginners as they give a more "finished" appearance to your work, without hours of fussy modeling.

Cutters (11)
Various cutters are used throughout the book. Basic shape cutters, such as a set of round and square cutters, are invaluable, as are flower cutters. Think about building up a collection of your favorite cutters.

Water Brush
This brush has its own reservoir of water behind the bristles to keep edible glue from drying out.

Foam Pad (12) ✪
You can use pads of foam to hold paste pieces in place until dry or as a work surface when using the tools to mold the paste.

Internal Supports/Dowels
Dried spaghetti strands or sugar sticks are edible and can provide internal support for models. Should support within the cake be required, plastic dowels can be used.

Spacers/Formers (13)
Spacers enable you to roll your paste to a uniform thickness. Place one spacer either side of the paste. When your rolling pin touches both spacers, the paste will have been rolled evenly.

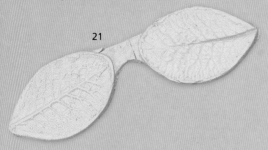

21

22

Cake Decorating Tools

Cake Drums (14)
Thick cake boards are called cake drums, and are used to support the cake and present it. Usually a drum that is 2 in. (5 cm) larger than the cake, and the same shape as the cake, is used. Sometimes, if decorative items are to be placed on the cake drum, such as models or flowers, then a larger drum can be used, and for a more contemporary look, a complementary cake drum shape can be used, such as an oval with a round cake. It is a good idea to have spare drums to hand, especially when preparing the cake.

Piping Bags (15)
Piping bags can be reusable or made from paper and are used to add frosting decoration to cakes.

Piping Bottles (16, 17)
An alternative to piping bags, piping bottles are handy for storing frostings to stop them from drying out.

Piping Tubes
Piping tubes or nozzles can be plastic or metal. The metal tubes are the best quality, will give a perfect result every time, and will not get damaged during the washing process. Don't forget to purchase a brush to clean the tubes properly. The large end of a piping tube is excellent for indenting a model with a smiling mouth.

Turntable
A turntable is extremely useful for creating the complete cake decoration, enabling you to work on the whole of the cake more easily. It may be on a pedestal that raises the cake up to assist in decoration, or flat so you can sit and work.

Cake Comb (18)
A cake comb will imprint patterns or lines onto your cake surface. Cake combs work well on buttercream.

Side Scriber/Marker (19)
You can change the height of the pin on a side scriber to get a line around the cake a uniform distance from the base. This assists in the equal application of frosting or frills.

17

16

19

15

18

Molds

Molds produce sugarcraft items that can be added to the cake or topper straight away, such as a "string of pearls," or may be left to dry first then added later.

Extruder (20)

The extruder is supplied with 12 disks, all with different shapes or holes stamped out that paste can be extruded through to create all sorts of decorative designs. The multihole disks also create wonderful hair for topper designs. The paste that is extruded must be mixed with shortening first to make it softer.

Veiners (21)

Veining petals or leaves can be made very much easier with specialized veiners; however, these do tend to be expensive. Invest in veiners that you know you will use frequently, or for items that might be difficult to do, such as a daffodil trumpet.

Crimpers (22)

Crimpers add texture and patterns to paste and can be bought in varying designs. These are fun, easy and quick to use.

Palette Knife (23)

Useful for all types of decorative techniques, from applying buttercream to carefully positioning a topper on your cake. Look out for good-quality large and small flat-bladed and cranked palette knives.

23

14

20

Basic Baking Equipment

Food Mixer (1)
Not essential, but a food mixer will make cake making less time consuming, and cakes tend to be better mixed and lighter.

Mixing Bowls (2)

Glass Measuring Cup (3)

Whisk (4)

Palette Knives (5)

Wooden Spoons

Plastic Spatula (6)

Sugar Shaker (7)
Ideal for shaking confectioners' sugar out for dusting the work surface.

Sieve (8)

Nonstick Rolling Pin and Workboard (9)

Textured Rolling Pin
These are quite expensive so make sure you consult a store attendant before buying. The silk-texture pin is particularly useful.

Pastry Brush (10)

Scissors (11)

Bakeware (12)

Cooling Rack (13)

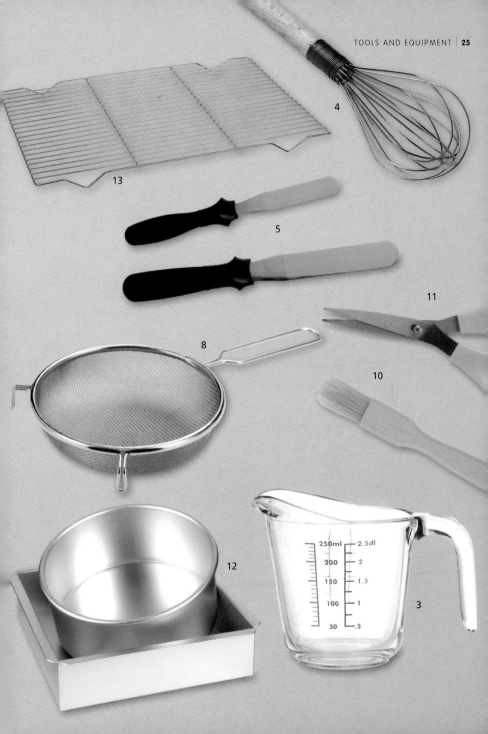

designing your cake

You have an important day coming up for a family member or friend... What better way to show your sugarcraft skills than by designing the perfect cake? Choose a theme that suits the occasion, and let your creative juices flow.

Planning Checklist
It is a good idea when planning a design to write a checklist of steps to follow to help you create a unique, inventive design.

1 Start with a strong theme—this might be decided by a customer—then list the ideas that go along with the theme (in this instance, riverbank); for example fish, frog, bulrushes, water lilies, etc.

2 Find source material for each element of the cake, such as Internet images—they are not going to be copied, but used as a source for ideas, so no copyright will be affected. Collect swatches of colors that you want to incorporate and draw out panels of side designs showing shapes and colors that might be suitable. Collect models if you can; this frog was so much easier to model with a child's plastic one to help.

3 Make up a picture board by sketching out your ideas, so that you can plan colors and materials. Decide on the shape of cake you want to create, maybe a classic shape—round or square—or one that complements the overall theme: with the use of a template, a cake can be cut into any shape.

Creating a Successful Design

A successful design is properly researched, planned and positioned. This results in a cake that is balanced, with complementing colors and elements that blend together well—like the cake opposite. Techniques used on the cake will be appropriate for the style and mediums used. The design is complete with no gaps, and all the elements flow across the cake. Larger elements will usually be positioned at the back, with smaller or more important elements at the front.

An unsuccessful cake design—like those designs shown above and below—has not been properly planned, and the elements have not been researched or placed correctly on the cake. Colors are too harsh or too pale, detracting from the overall appearance of the cake.

4 Draw out a rough outline of the cake to help plan the position and size of the elements, then draw in the various features—they don't have to be masterpieces. Color the elements on the drawing, testing various shades—better to get it wrong here than on the cake later. You probably won't be able to match your colors exactly with the relevant food colors; however, this will give you a good idea of the shades and intensities you require.

5 Sort out the food colors by blending colors together to build up to the color you need (see pages 54–57), then note down the proportions of each.

Designing an Easter Cake
The challenge here was to design an Easter cake. Here, we went for a contemporary look that incorporated eggs, bunnies and spring flowers. It is important to know your market when designing your cake. Easter is an occasion that is celebrated by people of all ages, so it is important, in this instance, to make the design appealing to children. Begin by drawing together source material—pictures of rabbits, chicks and Easter eggs. Find swatches of suitable colors—look in magazines, children's books, cards and on the Internet. Don't confine yourself to only a few ideas, consider all or anything you find, and keep any discarded material as it may come in handy next time.

Test various shades of color on a "mood board." Look for colors you like in ribbons or candy wrappers so that you can match the colors to the gum paste. Put thought into your design now and it will show in the final cake.

Experiment with composition. Try combining the elements of your cake in different ways. Add color in different combinations until you find the one that is right for your cake.

Sketch out ideas for the cake top to see what works. There may be a particular element that you are really good at creating, that you want to exhibit at its best. This drawing of a bunny in a plant pot influenced the whole design, but was discarded in favor of improved ideas for the final cake.

When you feel confident that you have considered all design options, draw out the finished cake, with elements in proportion, in color and in position. This is the last chance to make sure everything is working together.

Designing a Christening or "New Baby" Cake

The most important thing about designing a christening or "new baby" cake is to make it appropriate for the occasion, whether religious or non-religious. Pastel shades are a good choice, as are baby animals—like the elephants in this design. You may also want to include the baby's name or, in this instance, the word "BABY." As always, begin by collecting your materials: reference photos, font styles, color swatches, etc. Remember that you can merge your source materials. For example, you might take the body of the elephant from one photo and the ears from another to create a unique creature.

Less is more. Fewer colors in your cake will create a bolder effect. In the final design, we kept the cake and lettering the same color and used only three colors for the elephants.

The playful poses of the elephants are key to the cake's charm, so sketch out as many variations as you can before settling on your final design.

Choose an appropriate font that will work with your topper designs. See pages 82–85 for how to make and cut letter templates. You could use the extruder to make curly lettering, which would be fun for children, but here we settled for a clear and graphic font that acts as a "playground" for the elephant designs.

Choose appropriate elements to decorate the foreground of your cake. Avoid large or detailed designs that will detract from the message of the cake.

Draw out the cake top to get an idea of positioning and size. In this instance, it became apparent that the letters were too cluttered. Three elephants on the first three letters was too much. Moving an elephant to the letter "Y" (as in the final cake) made the design more balanced.

essential cake recipe

The cake topper must have a setting, so a cake is needed. Don't panic! Follow the recipe and instructions and you will have made the perfect cake for your topper. Various flavors of cake can be made with a little alteration to the basic recipe.

The first thing to decide is what size cake you need. This will depend on how many people are to eat it. The size guide (right) is based on pieces of cake that are 1 in. (2.5 cm) square, which is sufficient if the cake is to be served after a full meal. If the cake is to be used instead of the dessert, the slice size will need to be larger.

SIZE GUIDE		
SIZE OF CAKE	ROUND: NUMBER OF 1 IN. (2.5 CM) SQUARE PIECES FROM A ROUND CAKE	SQUARE: NUMBER OF 1 IN. (2.5 CM) SQUARE PIECES FROM A SQUARE CAKE
6 in. (15 cm)	10	20
7 in. (18 cm)	15	30
8 in. (20.5 cm)	20	45
9 in. (23 cm)	33	54
10 in. (25.5 cm)	40	60
11 in. (28 cm)	50	78
12 in. (30.5 cm)	60	90

Flavors

Citrus
Add the juice and zest of one fruit for every 2 tsp (10 ml) of vanilla extract in the recipe.

Chocolate
Add 1 oz. (30 g) for every 1 cup (250 ml) of flour. Add 1 tbsp (15 ml) milk for every 2 oz. (60 g).

Natural Vanilla
Use the seeds from one vanilla pod for the smaller cakes and two for the larger ones.

See also
Cake Frosting, pages 36–38 > Pastes, Icings, Glues, pages 39–43 > Preparing the Cake, pages 44–49

The perfect cake is moist throughout with a good texture, and not too crumbly.

Perfect Cake Recipe Chart

This recipe chart gives all the weights of ingredients required for each size of pan to produce a cake of good depth, around 3–3½ in. (7.5–9 cm). Always follow either imperial or metric measurements, since they are not interchangeable. If you mix them up, the resulting cake will be poor quality.

CLASSIC SPONGE CAKE RECIPE

ROUND PAN	6 in. (15 cm)	7 in. (18 cm)	8 in. (20.5 cm)	9 in. (23 cm)	10 in. (25.5 cm)	11 in. (28 cm)	12 in. (30.5 cm)	13 in. (33 cm)
SQUARE PAN	5 in. (12.5 cm)	6 in. (15 cm)	7 in. (18 cm)	8 in. (20.5 cm)	9 in. (23 cm)	10 in. (25.5 cm)	11 in. (28 cm)	12 in. (30.5 cm)
UNSALTED BUTTER	¾ cup (185 ml)	1 cup (250 ml)	1¾ cups (425 ml)	2¼ cups (560 ml)	3 cups (750 ml)	3⅓ cups (825 ml)	4⅛ cup (1.3 L)	4¾ cups (1.75 L)
CONFECTIONERS' SUGAR	1⅓ cups (325 ml)	2 cups (500 ml)	3¼ cups (810 ml)	4 cups (1 L)	5¼ cups (1.3 L)	6 cups (1.5 L)	7¼ cups (1.8 L)	8⅓ cups (2.08 L)
LARGE EGGS	3	4	7	8	10	11	13	14
SELF-RISING FLOUR	2 cups (500 ml)	3 cups (750 ml)	5 cups (1.25 ml)	6 cups (1.5 L)	8¾ cups (2.2 L)	10 cups (2.5 L)	11.5 cups (3 L)	12¼ cups (3.06 L)
MILK	1 tbsp (15 ml)	1 tbsp (15 ml)	1 tbsp (15 ml)	2 tbsp (30 ml)	2 tbsp (30 ml)	3 tbsp (45 ml)	3 tbsp (45 ml)	4 tbsp (60 ml)
VANILLA EXTRACT	½ tsp (2.5 ml)	1 tsp (5 ml)	2½ tsp (7.5 ml)	3 tsp (15 ml)	4 tsp (20 ml)	4 tsp (20 ml)	5½ tsp (27.5 ml)	6 tsp (30 ml)
BAKING TIME	½ hr	1 hr	1 hr 20 mins	1hr 40 mins	2 hrs	2 hrs 15 mins	2 hrs 30 mins	2 hrs 45 mins

Chocolate sponge is a favorite and works well with all types of frosting.

Making the Cake

Follow the instructions carefully when making your cake, paying particular attention to the addition of flour. Overbeating will make the cake heavy and dense.

1 Heat the oven to 350°F (180°C). Prepare the cake pan by greasing and lining the base and sides.

2 Beat softened butter and sugar together using a food mixer (or by hand if preferred) until light in color and fluffy.

3 Add one egg at a time and beat in thoroughly. If the mix looks as if it is splitting, add a teaspoon (5 ml) of flour. Add any flavorings now too (see Flavors, page 32).

4 Add the dry ingredients, sifting in a little at a time and folding in gently by hand using a metal spoon or a rubber spatula. Spoon the mixture carefully into the prepared pan, smooth the top, then leave slightly inverted in the center. Place on the middle shelf in the oven. Check the cake once, 15 minutes before the end of the cooking time, but don't be tempted to keep on looking, since if you keep opening the door the cake will sink.

5 Test the cake using a skewer or toothpick inserted into the deepest part. The skewer (or toothpick) should come out clean.

6 Allow the cake to cool for 30 minutes before turning out onto a cooling rack. Follow the instructions on pages 44–47 to further prepare the cake.

Five Tips for Happy Baking

- Heat the oven for 20 minutes before the cake goes in to ensure that the temperature will be at a constant from the start.
- Place the cake in the center of the oven, not touching the sides.
- Ensure all equipment for making and baking is grease-free.
- Always measure accurately, using only one set of measurements. Don't switch between imperial and metric.
- Always grease and line cake pans correctly; it saves so much frustration later.

TROUBLESHOOTING

• Cake sinks in the center
This is usually because the cake isn't cooked in the middle. Test the cake by inserting a skewer into the deepest part. If it comes out clean it is cooked, if not, give it a little longer. Sometimes overbeating the cake at the batter stage can over-aerate it; this will cause it to sink during or shortly after baking. Always make sure you follow the recipe proportions correctly.

• Domed/cracked top
This isn't really a problem since the cake can simply be leveled (see page 44). However, if when you fill the cake pan you make the center of the cake slightly lower than the edges, the cooked cake will have balanced out. The top has cracked because the outside of the cake has cooked more quickly than the center; the center then cooks and expands, cracking the top. A slightly cooler oven will allow the cake to cook at a more even rate.

• Grainy appearance and dry cake
The cake was not mixed sufficiently and may also have contained insufficient liquid. Milk can always be added if the mixture looks too dry.

• Cake is burned
The cake was left too long in the oven, or the oven is heating incorrectly. You may be able to resurrect the cake by cutting away the burned section, but take care that the flavor of the rest of the cake isn't affected.

• Cake is too heavy/dense
This is usually due to too much flour, or overmixing the flour, so take care not to cross-weigh using two different units of measurement. The oven could also be too hot, so if this is a recurring problem, an oven thermometer might be a worthwhile buy.

cake frosting

Cake frosting is any sweet, spreadable covering made of sugar, butter, water, egg whites or milk. It is often flavored, and sometimes cooked, and is used to fill, cover and sometimes decorate cakes.

There is a slight difference between the main types of frosting used in the United States and the United Kingdom, where it is usually called buttercream. However, both are soft and fluffy, very adaptable and add an extra-special element to an already delicious cake. The frosting can be spread using a palette knife, piped with various decorative piping tubes or textured using various patterns. It can also be used as an underlayer to other cake coatings, sticking the top coat to the cake.

Chocolate sponge covered in milk chocolate frosting creates a decadent treat.

Flavors and Colors

Cake frosting can be flavored with almost any flavor you care to use. Frosting flavors tend to complement the cake flavor, with the frosting flavor being more intense, for example chocolate cake with dark chocolate frosting. Alternatively, the frosting can add in another flavor that enriches that of the cake, such as a chocolate cake with a Morello cherry frosting, or vanilla cake with lavender and elderflower frosting.

Frosting, like any other cake covering, can be colored using the same food colors used for gum paste (see pages 54–59)—chocolate will naturally have its own color. Start with the basic frosting or buttercream recipes (shown opposite and over the page), then add the color.

If the thought of making the frosting is a little scary, or you are short of time, you can buy it ready-made from good food stores where it is marketed as American frosting, or make the buttercream recipe instead, which is very quick and straightforward.

Quantities

The table below gives quantities of frosting ingredients required for different cake sizes to allow for two layers of filling within the cake. The same quantity again would be required for covering the outside of the cake also.

HOW MUCH FROSTING/BUTTERCREAM?

SIZE OF CAKE	BUTTER	CONFECTIONERS' SUGAR
6 in. (15 cm)	¼ cup (60 ml)	1 cup (250 ml)
7 in. (18 cm)	⅓ cup (75 ml)	1⅓ cups (325 ml)
8 in. (20.5 cm)	½ cup (125 ml)	1¾ cups (435 ml)
9 in. (23 cm)	½ cup (125 ml)	1¾ cups (435 ml)
10 in. (25.5 cm)	¾ cup (185 ml)	2½ cups (375 ml)
11 in. (28 cm)	¾ cup (185 ml)	2½ cups (375 ml)
12 in. (30.5 cm)	1 cup (250 ml)	3 cups (750 ml)

Basic Frosting

This is a typical American recipe for a most delicious frosting. Although the technique is rather time-consuming in comparison to making buttercream, it is worth it. Bring all the ingredients to room temperature before you begin, and have the cake ready too.

INGREDIENTS
- **4 large eggs**
- **1 cup (250 ml) granulated sugar**
- **2 tsp (10 ml) vanilla extract or other flavoring**
- **2 cups (500 ml) unsalted butter, cut into small, walnut-sized pieces**
- **½ tsp (2.5 ml) salt**

1 In a mixing bowl, beat together the eggs, sugar and vanilla extract.

2 Find a saucepan that the mixing bowl can sit on without touching the bottom. Pour about 1 in. (2.5 cm) of water into the pan and bring to a boil. Reduce the heat to a simmer and place the mixing bowl over the water pot to form a double boiler. This will allow the eggs to heat up slowly and avoid them turning into scrambled egg.

3 Whisk continuously over the steaming water until the eggs reach 160°F (71°C) on a sugar thermometer.

4 Remove from the heat and beat the hot mixture until it cools to room temperature.

5 Beat in the butter one piece at a time until the frosting is smooth. If the mixture starts to look curdled, continue to beat until smooth.

Consistency
Do not add the butter too quickly, otherwise the frosting will go thick and greasy.

Storing Frosting

> The frosting will last in the fridge for up to six days or six months in a freezer. To reuse, make sure you warm the frosting up gradually, either over simmering water or in the microwave, beating as it starts to warm up. If you warm it up too quickly, put it back in the fridge for a while.

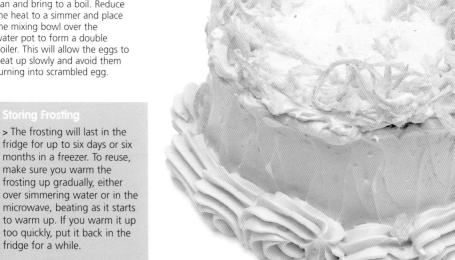

Buttercream

A traditional English recipe that uses equal quantities of butter and confectioners' sugar. For best results use a food mixer, although a wooden spoon will do too.

INGREDIENTS
- **1 cup (250 ml) unsalted butter, softened**
- **1¾ cups (435 ml) confectioners' sugar, sifted**
- **Flavoring (see Buttercream Flavors, below)**

1 Place the butter in a glass bowl and add the sifted confectioners' sugar, a little at a time, beating slowly as you go. Add your chosen flavoring.

2 Once all the sugar has been incorporated, continue to beat until light and fluffy.

Buttercream Flavors
- **Vanilla**
Add 2 tsp (10 ml) of vanilla extract or the seeds of one vanilla pod.

- **Citrus**
Add the juice and zest of one piece of fruit.

- **Coffee**
Add 2 tbsp (30 ml) of strong coffee.

- **Chocolate**
Add ¼ cup (60 ml) of good cocoa powder.

Storing Buttercream
> Store buttercream in an airtight container and place in the fridge until required. Beat again before using. Buttercream can be stored in the fridge for up to two weeks.

pastes, icings, glues

There are various paste and icing recipes to choose from when decorating your cakes.

Rolled Fondant

Rolled fondant and fondant icing (sugarpaste in the UK) are the same thing—not to be confused with poured fondant—and are used to decorate cakes. This paste is made using gelatin (or agar in vegetarian recipes) and glycerine, which keep the sugar malleable and create a dough-like consistency, so it can be rolled out like pastry and used to cover cakes. This covering gives cakes a smooth, silky appearance.

Using store-bought rolled fondant, which is available from specialist stores, saves time, and the consistency of the paste is constant and much less likely to crack and dry. If you prefer to make your own, or have difficulty obtaining rolled fondant, this recipe makes 15½ cups (4 L).

INGREDIENTS
- **2 packets (8 tsp/40 ml) gelatin**
- **½ cup (125 ml) cold water**
- **2 tbsp (30 ml) glycerine**
- **1 cup (250 ml) liquid glucose**
- **15½ cups (4 L) confectioners' sugar plus extra for dusting**

1 Sprinkle the gelatin over the cold water in a bowl and let it soak until it is spongy.

2 Stand the bowl over boiled water and stir until the gelatin dissolves.

3 Stir in the glycerine and glucose.

4 Sift 15½ cups (4 L) of the confectioners' sugar into a bowl and make a well in the center.

5 Slowly pour in the liquid, constantly stirring. Mix well.

6 Pour the fondant onto a work surface that has been well dusted with confectioners' sugar and knead until smooth.

Coloring Tip
When coloring rolled fondant, use paste food colors that will not alter its consistency. If you need to use liquid food colors, more confectioners' sugar may be required to reduce the stickiness of the paste.

Sprinkle gelatin over the cold water (see Step 1).

Storing Rolled Fondant

> Keep rolled fondant in an airtight bag or container since it will dry out quickly and become crumbly. This will cause lumps in the paste, damaging the smooth effect required for a professional-looking covered cake.

Gum paste

Also known as modeling paste or Mexican modeling paste, gum paste is a nonsticky medium for making sugar models. It can be creased, folded and textured without cracking and is perfect for beginners because it doesn't dry out too quickly. If it is supported while it dries, using foam, the piece will keep its shape. However, while it is dry and firm on the outside, it is still soft inside, making it perfect for cakes for children.

A ready-made gum paste is ideal in consistency in that it isn't too hard to work with and holds itself well, needing little support. This is a huge advantage when making complex models.

Using Gum Tragacanth

If you cannot find ready-made gum paste, you can make your own by mixing food-grade gum tragacanth or tylose powder with rolled fondant.

It takes one hour to start working, but is even better left overnight. Alternatively, follow the recipe for flower paste (opposite), and mix equal amounts of flower paste and rolled fondant to give an excellent gum paste.

If the paste is too dry...

Should the paste become dry, either by being exposed to air for too long or by mixing it with too much cornstarch—used to stop the paste sticking—work a small amount of shortening into the paste.

If the paste is too wet...

To stiffen gum paste, add gum tragacanth, a little at a time, until the right consistency is achieved.

INGREDIENTS
- **1 tsp (5 ml) gum tragacanth/ 1 tsp (5 ml) tylose powder**
- **8 oz. (225 g) fondant**

1 Sprinkle 1 tsp gum tragacanth onto your work surface.

2 Knead the fondant on the work surface until all the powder is incorporated.

Storing Gum Paste

> Keep your paste sealed in a plastic bag or plastic wrap when not in use to ensure it doesn't dry out.

Flower Paste

Flower paste (also known as floral paste or petal paste) is a soft, malleable paste that sets very firmly when left to dry in air. It is perfect for making flowers because it holds its shape well, so it can be rolled out very thinly to make delicate petals or leaves. It is nonsticky and works well with molds and veiners.

Flower paste is available in various colors, although you can color the basic white and cream varieties using paste colors.

A delicate flower is easily achieved using flower paste—which will stand up to being rolled thinly.

INGREDIENTS
- **1 tsp (5 ml) gelatin**
- **1 tsp (5 ml) shortening**
- **5 tsp (25 ml) cold water**
- **1¾ cups (435 ml) confectioners' sugar**

1 Place the gelatin, shortening and water in a small, heavy-based pan and heat gently until the shortening and gelatin dissolve and the liquid is clear.

2 Gradually stir in the confectioners' sugar until the mixture forms a ball.

3 Knead in the remaining confectioners' sugar (add a little more confectioners' sugar if necessary) until the flower paste is smooth and pliable.

Storing Flower Paste
> Always keep flower paste in a plastic bag so that it does not dry out. Flower paste doesn't require refrigeration and can be kept for up to six months in the freezer.

Marzipan

Marzipan (or almond paste) is a soft, malleable paste that is used most frequently to cover a fruit cake before it is iced. It is primarily made from almonds and sugar, and is readily available from supermarkets. It is also a perfect medium for modeling, especially for the beginner, because it is easy to mold into an impressive model.

A ready-made almond paste is good for modeling because it is a little firmer than most other marzipans and excellent at holding its shape. Softer marzipan is perfect for covering cakes, although nothing can beat the taste of homemade marzipan. When making your own paste, different flavors can be added to complement the cake flavor.

Caution
Marzipan contains raw egg, so make sure you use only pasteurized eggs that are salmonella free, otherwise it should not be given to anyone in an at-risk group.

INGREDIENTS
- **¾ cup (185 ml) golden superfine sugar**
- **2¼ cups (560 ml) confectioners' sugar, sifted, plus extra for dusting**
- **5¼ cups (1.3 L) ground almonds**
- **Flavoring, such as the seeds from a vanilla pod or 2 tsp (10 ml) of rum (a little extra confectioners' sugar will be needed)**
- **2 eggs, beaten**

1 Place the sugars and ground almonds in a large bowl.

2 Rub in the vanilla seeds or add the rum.

3 Make a well in the middle of the bowl, add the eggs and blend using a knife.

4 Dust the work surface with confectioners' sugar and knead the marzipan to a smooth dough. Don't overdo the kneading since this will make the marzipan greasy. Add more confectioners' sugar if the paste becomes too sticky.

Storing Marzipan
> Wrap marzipan in a plastic bag and keep in a cool place. Marzipan can be made up to two days in advance, and can be kept for up to a week. If used as a covering, once the cake is covered and given sufficient time to dry, it will last for up to two months.

Modeling chocolate is a versatile medium that is ideal for creating delicate features such as the feathers on this parrot topper.

Modeling Chocolate

Like marzipan, modeling chocolate is an excellent medium to use for decorative models, from flowers on a wedding cake to animals on a birthday cake. It is available in three main colors: dark, milk and white. They are made from delicious Belgian chocolate and give a wonderful creamy flavor. The white modeling chocolate can be colored any shade you can imagine.

Tips for Using Modeling Chocolate

- Don't knead it too much, since it will become very sticky and unusable.
- When adding color, blend for the shortest time possible then leave in a plastic bag for a while to cool down and firm up.
- When making flowers or petals, roll the chocolate between two pieces of plastic—a plastic folder is ideal—to prevent the chocolate from becoming too warm and sticky, and to ensure there are no fingermarks.

- When softening modeling chocolate on a foam pad, press gently.
- Modeling chocolate will stick to itself without any glue or water to assist.
- Modeling chocolate will stay soft and malleable for a while, so pieces on a model will require support.

Royal Icing

Royal icing is a hard white icing traditionally used on Christmas cakes and wedding cakes. When modeling, it can be used as an excellent "glue" to help attach large or heavy pieces. It can be textured into peaks, smoothed out to give a perfectly flat surface and piped into amazing shapes, such as coils, lines, shells and flowers, and is sometimes used for hair on figures.

Royal icing can be bought ready-made, but it is easy to make at home using a food mixer, confectioners' sugar and egg white or egg white substitute, with a little glycerine to stop it turning rock-hard. Egg substitute or fortified albumen, made into a liquid following the manufacturer's instructions, is a safer option than egg white, although the flavor is different.

Storing Royal Icing

> Cover the surface of the icing with a damp sheet of paper towel or plastic wrap. This will stop the icing from crusting and blocking a piping tube. Royal icing lasts two days. Do not refrigerate unless placed in an airtight container.

INGREDIENTS
- **2 large egg whites or egg white substitute made up following the manufacturer's instructions**
- **1¾ cups (435 ml) confectioners' sugar, sifted**
- **2 tsp (10 ml) glycerine**

1 First ensure the bowl of the food mixer is thoroughly clean and grease-free. Beat the egg liquid for one minute.

2 Add a tablespoon of confectioners' sugar at a time and beat in well.

3 Once all the sugar has been added, beat for a further minute, until sleek and shiny.

4 Add the glycerine and beat for a further minute.

5 Test the consistency of the icing. A cake coating needs to be softer than icing for piping or decorative work in order to keep its shape.

Piping Gel
Piping gel is available store-bought and cannot be made. It is commonly used to soften royal icing and to stop it from drying out too quickly. It can also be painted directly onto gum paste, giving a "wet" look when dry. See the cauldron on page 161 for a good example of this effect.

Edible Glue
This quick and simple recipe makes an excellent glue for fixing parts of a model together. Ready-made edible glue can be purchased and works equally well. When making your own glue, ensure you use boiled water to remove any bacteria or fungus that might contaminate it and keep in a screw-topped jar. Apply using a clean paintbrush.

INGREDIENTS
- **½ tsp (2.5 ml) gum tragacanth**
- **3 tbsp (45 ml) boiled water**

1 Sprinkle the gum tragacanth powder over the warm water and mix.

2 Leave until the powder is absorbed, then mix again. The mixture should be clear. The glue will be smooth, without lumps, and have a soft consistency. If the glue thickens or is too thick for your needs, add a little more boiled water.

Storing Edible Glue
> Store in a screw-top jar. Use within a month.

Sugar Sticks
These are made from flower paste and dried to use as supports in some models. If you don't have time to dry them, dried spaghetti strands are just as good. Although both sugar sticks and dried spaghetti are edible, sugar sticks are more tasty and should be used for children. For demonstration purposes, dried spaghetti is used throughout the topper directory.

INGREDIENTS
- **Flower paste**
- **½ tsp (2.5 ml) shortening**

1 Take a small amount of flower paste, add a little shortening and work in to soften the paste.

2 Extrude through an extruder with a medium-hole disk, making a long, thin string of paste.

3 Cut into long, medium and short lengths ready for different applications.

4 Dry flat on hard foam, rolling periodically to dry evenly.

Storing Sugar Sticks
> Store sugar sticks in a cool, dry place, until required. If kept in a plastic bag, sugar sticks can be used indefinitely.

preparing the cake

Preparing the cake should always come before you start to make your toppers, especially since in some cases the topper needs to be added to the cake before the topper dries, so that it can mold to the cake shape; for example, a figure sitting on the edge of a cake.

Leveling

Ideally, a cake with a depth of 3–3½ in. (7.5–9 cm) is the perfect size to work with, because it allows for leveling without making the cake too shallow. The leveling process involves cutting away the domed top of the cake to give a nice flat surface.

Tools

- Sponge cake (see pages 32–35)
- Ruler
- Side scriber
- Long serrated knife
- Wax paper
- Spirit level
- Turntable (optional)

1 Measure the height of the side of the cake at its lowest point.

2 Alter the height of the side scriber to this height and scribe a line all the way around the cake.

See also
Essential Cake Recipe, pages 32–35 > Cake Frosting, pages 36–38 > Piping Techniques, pages 50–53

Turning the cake over so that the base is the top of the cake, gives you a smooth surface that is flat and easy to cover.

Syrup Flavors
If you have made a flavored cake, you may wish to further complement the cake with a flavored syrup, available from Internet suppliers. The syrup flavors are too delicate to survive the baking process, but are excellent when added after the cake has been baked, either sprinkled on the baked sponge or used in the filling.

3 Use the long serrated knife to indent this line, and continue cutting deeper into the cake until the excess has been removed. Turn over so that the base is the top of the cake.

4 Place wax paper on the cake and the spirit level on top of that to check that the cake is level. If it is not, carefully trim a little away from the raised point.

Filling

The delicious cake, carefully sliced (and perhaps sprinkled with syrup), is ready for filling. Follow the instructions on pages 37–38 to prepare your chosen filling of basic frosting or buttercream.

Tools: Filling

- Leveled sponge cake (see previous page)
- Cake drum
- Large and small palette knives

- Basic frosting or buttercream (see pages 37–38)
- Fruit jelly (optional)

1 Transfer the top layer of the cake (originally the base of the cake) to a spare cake drum and use a palette knife to spread frosting or buttercream over the cake, ensuring you spread evenly over the whole layer. If you are using it, spread fruit jelly over the filling.

2 Stack the top layer on top by sliding it gradually onto the layer of filling. If you are making a three-layer cake, then repeat the same filling process, remembering not to press too hard when spreading the filling.

Covering with Frosting

Frosting, whether American frosting or buttercream, makes a delicious covering for a cake, and can be colored to match the theme of the celebration or its decoration. It can also be piped, swirled and textured.

The first application of frosting is known as a "crumb coat," and is a thin layer of frosting that sticks any loose crumbs to the cake, ensuring that the second and final layer is not spoiled by crumbs.

1 Use the palette knife to spread the frosting thinly and smoothly over the top of the cake first, then the sides of the cake. Place the cake in the fridge to chill.

Tools: Covering with Frosting

- Filled sponge cake (see above)
- Basic frosting or buttercream (see pages 37–38)
- Palette knife
- Straight-edge ruler
- Cake comb (see below)
- Large piping bag and tube

2 Spread the next layer of frosting over the top of the cake. Draw the straight-edge rule across the top of the cake, paddling back and forth, then scrape gently but smoothly in one direction to leave a smooth top. You can rechill and reapply if you want a thicker layer.

3 If you are using a cake comb to leave a pattern, use this now in the soft frosting and chill again.

4 Fill a large piping bag with a large tube with frosting (see pages 50–51) and pipe around the edge of the cake, covering the join. Pipe around the base of the cake also, if desired.

Covering with Rolled Fondant

Covering a cake with rolled fondant gives it a smooth, firm surface. The technique shown in the sequence below is used to cover the cake drum, and to cover a cake with marzipan.

Before You Begin

Place the cake on a spare cake drum—you will need to cover the actual cake drum with paste before positioning the cake (see opposite). Just before you are about to roll out the paste for cake covering, cover the cake again with a very thin layer of frosting, which will adhere the paste to the cake (see pages 46–47).

Tools

- Workboard
- Confectioners' sugar
- Rolled fondant (see right for quantities)
- Large acrylic rolling pin
- Filled sponge cake
- Pin
- Palette knife
- Cake smoother
- Cake drum
- Pastry brush
- Boiled and cooled water

HOW MUCH ROLLED FONDANT?

SIZE OF CAKE	CAKE COVERING	DRUM COVERING
5 in. (12.5 cm) round	14 oz. (400 g)	–
5 in. (12.5 cm) square / 6 in. (15 cm) round	1lb, 2 oz. (500 g)	–
6 in. (15 cm) square / 7 in. (18 cm) round	1lb, 11 oz. (770 g)	4 oz. (115 g)
7 in. (18 cm) square / 8 in. (20.5 cm) round	1lb, 14 oz. (875 g)	4½ oz. (130 g)
8 in. (20.5 cm) square / 9 in. (23 cm) round	2lb, 3 oz. (1 kg)	6 oz. (170 g)
9 in. (23 cm) square / 10 in. (25.5 cm) round	2lb, 12 oz. (1.25 kg)	8 oz. (225 g)
10 in. (25.5 cm) square / 11 in. (28 cm) round	3lb, 5 oz. (1.5 kg)	10½ oz. (305 g)
11 in. (28 cm) square / 12 in. (30.5 cm) round	3lb, 10 oz. (1.75 kg)	13 oz. (370 g)
12 in. (30.5 cm) square	4lb, 13 oz. (2.2 kg)	1 lb (450 g)

1 Dust the workboard with confectioners' sugar. Knead the rolled fondant until it is soft and smooth. Roll out the paste to a thickness of around ¾ in. (2 cm) using the rolling pin. Keep in mind the overall shape you require, rolling to approximately this shape.

2 Use the rolling pin to lift the paste onto the cake, making sure you have it positioned correctly. This method should prevent air getting trapped underneath the paste, which will cause a bubble in the icing—if you do get a bubble, prick the hole with a fine pin and gently smooth the air out.

3 Start smoothing with your hands first to generally attach the paste to the cake. Smooth down the sides of the cake gently, taking care around the base and edge of the cake not to pull the paste and tear it. Roughly trim away excess paste with the palette knife.

Use the cake smoother to smooth the top of the cake first, then work around the sides. Trim further paste away neatly using the palette knife. Use the sharp edge of the cake smoother to give a neat finish to the base of the cake. Leave the cake to dry for a few hours.

4 If using marzipan, leave to dry for 24–48 hours. For rolled fondant, continue by smoothing a pad of paste over the cake, paying particular attention to the edges. Smoothing with the pad will even out the surface, bring together any slight tears in the paste, and remove any stray grains of sugar.

Covering a Cake Drum

1 To prepare the cake drum, use the pastry brush to brush a little cooled boiled water over the drum to help the paste adhere. Roll the paste over the rolling pin and lift onto the cake drum. Use the cake smoother to smooth the paste.

2 Trim around the edge of the cake drum, removing the excess paste, ensuring you don't cut in, but angle the palette knife outward.

3 Use a pad of paste to polish the cake drum further, removing excess confectioners' sugar and improving the surface.

4 Use the long palette knife to carefully transfer the covered cake onto the prepared cake drum.

piping techniques

Piping, as a decorative skill, is invaluable. It enables you to write inscriptions, neaten edges and add decorative flowers, dots, lines, coils and swirls. Buttercream and royal icing are perfect for piping.

Tools

• Wax or parchment paper
• Scissors

How to Make a Piping Bag

Ready-made greaseproof piping bags can be bought from specialist shops, and plastic piping bags are available on a roll; however, being able to make your own piping bag is a useful skill.

1 Cut out a square of wax or parchment paper and fold in half to make a double-layered triangle. Coil the outer points, one at a time, to the center point, making the center of the long side into the pointed end of the bag.

2 Fold the ends over to keep the bag in shape.

Filling and Using a Piping Bag

1 Hold the piping bag in your left hand. Use a palette knife to fill the bag half to two-thirds full with royal icing. (This will depend on the consistency of the icing and the size of the tip.) For very fine tips it is best to use only small amounts of icing.

2 With your thumb, push down the icing in the bag so that it eases into the piping tip. Next, fold the sides of the bag in toward the center. Keep pushing the icing down into the bag as you then fold over the top of the bag, making it tight.

3 Hold the piping bag between your thumb and index fingers and push down on the icing with your thumb. Place the pointed end of the tip in position over the work before beginning to push the icing through the bag.

Piping Tips
- Pressing with and releasing your thumb will cause the icing to flow and then stop. The icing will continue to flow after the pressure has stopped; therefore you must release pressure on the bag before you reach the end of piping a line. You will soon learn how to judge the pressure and movement required to produce the desired effects.

- Wipe the tube tip from time to time to ensure that the icing produces a good starting point. When not using the filled bag, simply wrap or stand the pointed end of the bag in a damp sponge or cloth.

Piping Effects

Piping tips are usually made of nickel, although plastic can also be used. They are seamless, thus aiding the flow of icing. Piping tips are numbered to identify their function. For piping lines, beads, dots and inscriptions, use No. 00–3. Choose No. 69–73 to pipe leaves and larger pieces. Always clean piping tips with hot, soapy water.

No. 1 round

Snail Trail

A fine piped snail trail is wonderful for tidying the join between the base of a cake and board without adding bulk or detracting from other elements of a cake design.

No. 1 round

Beads

A series of piped dots or beads can be used in the same way as a snail trail. A slightly damp paintbrush is useful for smoothing down lift-off marks on each bead.

Rope No. 43

Small Shell Border

A fine shell border is piped with fine to medium rope tips. The border is decorative without overpowering the general design of the cake.

Rope No. 43

Alternating Shells

Alternating and linking a series of piped shells using a rope, shell or star tip can create a decorative border suitable for the top or bottom edge of a royal-iced cake.

See also
Cake Frosting, pages 36–38 > Pastes, Icings, Glues, pages 39–43 > Preparing the Cake, pages 44–49

Large shell
No. 13

Ornate Shells
A large piped shell border can easily be transformed by adding overpiping or, as pictured here, with a series of dots piped with a small round piping tip.

Rope No. 43

S and C Scrolls
A shaky hand helps to add a rippled texture that complements this style of decoration. Use rope or shell tips.

Star No. 7

No. 1 round

Stars
Control is needed to pipe stars that are equal in size and height. A fine damp paintbrush is useful for tidying up take-off marks. Here the stars have been highlighted with small pink dots using a small round piping tip.

Leaf tip ST52

No. 1 round

Trailing Leaves
A wavy line piped with a small round piping tip forms the basic trailing stem, onto which a series of equal- or graduating-sized piped leaves is added using a specialty leaf tip. The icing needs to be firm to produce neat shapes. Embroidery-style flowers soften the effect.

Paste colors are concentrated, giving you a wide range of colors from pale to deep.

working with color

Color is crucial to successful cake toppers, and there is a huge range of coloring mediums available on the market. Color can be blended into frostings or pastes before you begin decorating or modeling, and can also be added afterward by painting or dusting—or both—with dusting powders that further enhance color and add depth.

Sourcing Food Colorings

Color can be added as a paste, a liquid or a powder. All can be used for various mediums, depending on what application is being considered.

• **Paste colors** have the widest choice of shades and give depth of color without making the gum paste or rolled fondant sticky. Make sure you replace the top on the paste color quickly to ensure it does not dry out.

Powders come in basic colors that are easily mixed to create a broad range.

• **Liquid colors** are available in a wide range of shades and are frequently used for airbrushing, or when absolute accuracy is required and drops need to be counted.

• **Powders** are available in various types and are used when adding further liquid would alter the consistency of the paste. Powders can be dusted onto previously colored and dried paste to enhance the existing color, or they can be mixed with vodka or cocoa butter to make paints that can be applied to the dried paste.

Color Strength

When adding color to paste, add it gradually, building up the strength of color in the paste. If you add too much and end up with a paste that is too dark, take some of the dark paste and add it to an equal amount of white paste to reduce the depth of color.

Liquid color can make pastes too sticky, so take care.

Coloring Paste

There are many, many colors you can make, just by mixing one colored paste with another. We show you how to mix colors below, and over the page we feature some of the many different colors you can create. Use disposable plastic gloves—available from most sugarcraft or housewares stores—when coloring dark paste, since these stop your fingers from being stained for days afterward.

1 Remove a small amount of frosting, gum paste or rolled fondant.

2 Take a clean toothpick, dip the end into the color and add this color to your paste.

3 Knead the paste to blend the color evenly. It is better to add the color gradually to achieve the color you require.

4 Place the colored paste in a plastic bag to stop it from drying out.

Mixing colors

Paste, liquid and powder colors come in a huge range, but occasionally the ideal color is just not available. Mixing two colors together may be the answer, or add white to create a pastel shade. Mixing can also be useful if you need only a small amount and it saves you from buying another color.

Understanding the Color Wheel

Using the principles behind an artist's color wheel can be helpful as it lets you plan a color scheme for your cake and cake topper. It helps you to select the correct colored pastes to mix together if you are trying to make a third color. The color wheel is made up of primary, secondary and tertiary colors (see below).

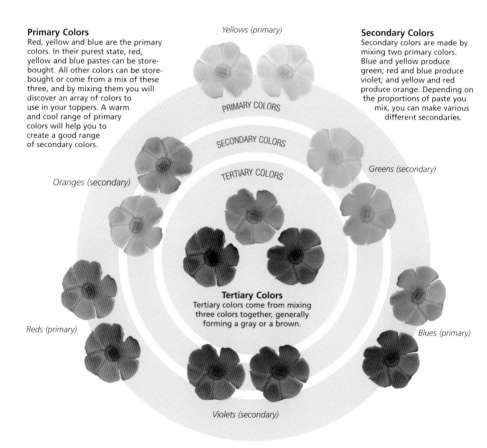

Primary Colors

Red, yellow and blue are the primary colors. In their purest state, red, yellow and blue pastes can be store-bought. All other colors can be store-bought or come from a mix of these three, and by mixing them you will discover an array of colors to use in your toppers. A warm and cool range of primary colors will help you to create a good range of secondary colors.

Secondary Colors

Secondary colors are made by mixing two primary colors. Blue and yellow produce green; red and blue produce violet; and yellow and red produce orange. Depending on the proportions of paste you mix, you can make various different secondaries.

Yellows (primary)

PRIMARY COLORS

SECONDARY COLORS

TERTIARY COLORS

Oranges (secondary)

Greens (secondary)

Tertiary Colors

Tertiary colors come from mixing three colors together, generally forming a gray or a brown.

Reds (primary)

Blues (primary)

Violets (secondary)

Color Schemes

The colors that are close together on the color wheel are said to be related, or harmonious. Harmonious colors go well together. A color scheme of blues and greens or one of pinks and violets would be called harmonious.

Colors opposite each other on the color wheel are rather confusingly called complementary colors. When complementary colors are placed side-by-side in a topper, they form bright, eye-catching contrasts. The red and green of the holly leaves and berries on page 132 has this effect.

Mixing Colored Pastes

Mixing colors close to each other on the color wheel makes a subtle variation. For example, mixing green and yellow paste together would give a lime green color.

Mixing opposites on the wheel (generally a primary and a secondary color, hence known as a tertiary color) creates neutral browns or grays. Brown pastes can be mixed in this way or there are ready-made browns available to buy.

White is an absence of color, and black is a collection of the three primary colors in intense form. It is easiest to buy black paste rather than trying to mix it. It will take a lot of color to turn the paste black and you will end up with disgusting fingernails. White paste should be store-bought.

Manipulating Colors

If you want to create a pastel-colored topper, start with soft-colored pastes. A hot pink and a bright yellow will not produce a soft apricot, unless you add plenty of white paste. Instead, start with a soft color, and add pinches of white until you reach the required color.

Essentially, if you mix two colored pastes together to create a further colored paste, the result will be muted. This can create some fabulous colors, such as moss green and dusky pink (see below). If you want to darken a color, don't add black as this will make the color murky. Instead, use the theory from the color wheel. For example, mix a pale red with a pale green (complementary colors on the color wheel since they are opposite each other). The outcome will create a dusky pink.

Pink + Pale green = Dusky rose

Leaf green + Orange = Moss green

Experiment to create skin tones

Skin tones are the most difficult colors to create. You'll learn by trial and error, so experiment. Record your results and keep blending until you find the tone you are after.

Start with white and cool red to make pastel pink	Start with white and orange to make pastel orange	Start with warm brown	Start with dark brown
+ Extra white and a touch of cool yellow =	+ Extra white and a touch of cool red =	+ Touch of violet =	+ Touches of dark violet and dark blue =
ROSE SKIN TONE	GOLDEN SKIN TONE	MID-TONED SKIN TONE	DARK SKIN TONE

Coloring with Dusting Powders

Dusting powders add shade and depth to dried icings and toppers. A powder can be added in small amounts to specific areas, for example, to deepen the color, highlight a petal or add pink cheeks to a figure, or it can be added over a large area to give the whole section a sparkle.

There are various powders available on the Internet, including specialist luster, iridescent and metallic dusting powders. More than one luster powder can be used in the same area, whether harmonious or contrasting, to add further depth and realism to the design you are creating.

Tools

- Dry paste topper
- Paintbrushes: small for delicate work or fanned for larger areas
- Palette
- Dusting powders
- Paper towels
- Vodka

1 Prepare the area to be dusted by first dusting with a dry brush to remove any leftover cornstarch.

Lift a small amount of dusting powder from the pot and onto the paper towel using a paintbrush.

2 Load the brush by working the powder into it from the paper towel. Don't put too much on since it can't be removed from the paste afterward.

3 Apply to the area in light strokes, building up the color.

Dusting Tips

> Never be tempted to add color to the item directly from the powder pot, since the color will be too deep and too much powder will fall off the brush when applied, spoiling areas where dust is not required.

> If you are concerned about flecks of powder falling onto particular parts of the cake, place a paper towel to mask these areas.

Making a Colored Paint

Painting a color onto your topper, especially when using silver or gold, is best done using powder color and vodka. The powder immediately turns to a liquid but dries almost instantly when applied to your topper.

1 Place a small amount of powder in the palette using a brush.

2 Add drops of vodka and mix with the powder to create a thin paste.

3 Apply to the topper using a paintbrush. If the paint starts to thicken, add further drops of vodka.

Author's Choice

Available to buy online, Squires Professional Double Strength Food Colors have been carefully tested and don't contain any harmful E numbers. Squires makes various ranges of colors, from the basic beginner selections to designer colors. All their colors are glycerine-free, and therefore are safe to use for runouts and sugar flowers, where complete drying is crucial.

working with gum paste

Gum paste is a fantastic medium to use for making the toppers in this book. It is easy to work with, whether you are a beginner or an expert. The paste will hold its shape, can be easily textured and allows the modeler to take their time in creating a masterpiece. The paste dries well but stays soft inside. When colored with paste colorings, its consistency is unaffected, and should you require a firmer paste for a support piece, further gum tragacanth can be blended with it, or use a stronger paste such as flower paste.

Tools

- Workboard
- Cornstarch
- Gum paste
- Acrylic rolling pin
- Pizza wheel
- Kemper knife
- Cutters
- Edible glue
- Paintbrush
- Royal icing
- Dried spaghetti or sugar sticks
- Foam pad
- Toothpick
- Flower veining tool

Rolling Paste

Gum paste is straightforward to roll. It is soft and will not crack when rolled out; however, if you do keep rerolling the paste, it will ultimately dry out as it takes in the cornstarch from the board. If this should happen, knead in a little shortening to moisten.

1 Lightly dust the workboard with the cornstarch, then knead the paste a little to get a smooth surface to roll out.

2 Roll out the chosen amount of paste carefully, using the rolling pin, rolling only a few times before moving the paste. This will ensure the paste will not stick to the board.

Cutting Paste Using a Pizza Wheel

The pizza wheel is possibly the best tool to use because it does not tempt you to pull the paste.

Dust the workboard and roll out the paste to the required thickness. Follow the line of the template with the blade of the pizza wheel.

Work slowly and carefully when working with fussy designs.

Cutting Paste Using a Knife

Paste yields easily to a knife. It is always best to use the sharpest knife you can to avoid tearing the paste.

Roll out the paste to the required thickness. If cutting around a template, cut in straight lines, then carefully trim around curves. Use the side of the Kemper knife to neaten curves.

Shaping Paste

Gum paste is shaped easily using fingers or simple tools. It yields well to light pressure from various tools, leading to perfect texturing and crack-free presentation. For advice on molding specific shapes, see pages 64–67.

Knead the paste lightly to make the surface smooth. Shape the paste using fingers or the flower veining tool.

Using Cutters

Cutters are available in an inexhaustible supply, whether you are after standard shapes, such as circles, squares or hexagons, or coils, swirls or character cutters for any number of themes. Flower cutters are plentiful, not only for the flowers but for the leaves too.

Follow the same principles when using cutters as when cutting with a pizza wheel or exacto knife, aiming to cut smoothly and straight down without tearing the paste. Cut out only what you need to work with at the time and cover the remaining paste, otherwise it will dry too much.

Attaching Paste Shapes

There are three possible techniques for attaching gum paste. Sometimes it is necessary to use two methods to ensure the topper will not collapse.

Using Edible Glue
One method is to lightly brush one side of the two pieces to be attached with edible glue. A paintbrush is adequate for this. The poor man's equivalent of edible glue is water, but it is not as strong a fixative as edible glue.

Using Royal Icing
The second method is to use royal icing, which is a little stronger than water. Apply a few dots of royal icing using a brush or Kemper knife and press the pieces together for a few minutes, or until the icing begins to set.

Using Sugar Sticks
This technique is usually applied when larger, heavier pieces of paste are being joined. First push a sugar stick (or dried spaghetti strand) into one paste piece, then dab with edible glue or water...

... and push the two pieces together.

These teddy heads require a support of dried spaghetti (or one or two sugar sticks) or they will topple over.

Layering
Layered pieces are attached only at one end, leaving the other end to be frilled or textured, accentuating the layering effect. This is often used when making side frills for cakes or frilled and textured clothes.

1 Prepare the first layer of paste by rolling, cutting and trimming. Place the paste on the foam pad with the end to be frilled at the edge of the pad. Rub a toothpick right and left over the paste, thinning and stretching it. The paste will curl up.

2 Use the flower veining tool over the upper part of the paste to indent light creases and create more of a fabric effect. Prepare the second, shorter layer in the same way.

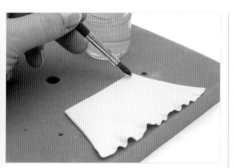

3 Lightly dampen the top of the lower layer, then place the second layer on top, aligned at the top.

4 Move the item to a workboard. The joined area can now be textured using the stitch embossing tool.

See also
Essential Shapes, pages 64–67 > Making Basic Figures, pages 68–73 > Texturing, pages 74–81

essential shapes

All the cake toppers in this book start out as basic shapes, and only then need a little tweaking to add the necessary details to change the basic shape into a unique topper. Start by practicing some of these shapes, particularly as a beginner, to build up confidence with the paste, working it with your fingers and various tools to see the effects. Don't worry about fingermarks; once you have the shape, the fingermarks can be lightly polished out.

Tools

- Cornstarch pad (for dusting)
- Workboard
- Gum paste
- Two cake smoothers
- Flower veining tool
- Exacto knife

BALL

The ball is ideal for heads, snowballs, eyes and pumpkins.

1 Dust the workboard and knead the paste a little to give a smooth surface.

2 Dust one of your palms with cornstarch, especially if your hands are warm,

then roll the paste carefully between both palms.

3 Continue to roll the paste until you have a smooth, round shape.

CUBE

A cube can be used for building blocks or books.

1 Dust the workboard and knead the paste until smooth.

2 Flatten the paste on four sides to create a rough cube shape.

3 Pinch each corner into a sharp point, but don't

indent the flat surface of the cube.

4 To avoid leaving fingermarks, use two cake smoothers to flatten two surfaces at a time, moving the cube over and flattening the next two sides until finished.

TEARDROP

A teardrop makes an elephant head and body, the center of a rose and cat ears.

1 Dust the workboard and knead the paste.

2 Dust one palm with cornstarch and roll the paste in your palms to form a ball.

3 Bring the paste forward to the edge of your palm and roll again, narrowing and pulling one end into the teardrop shape.

CONE

A cone is perfect for a snowman's nose.

1 Dust the workboard and knead the paste until smooth.

2 Dust one palm with cornstarch and roll the paste in the palm of your hands to form a ball.

3 Bring the paste forward in your palm and roll it on the edge of the hand, pulling one end into a teardrop.

4 Flatten the broad end to create the cone shape.

PYRAMID

A pyramid shape makes a good pumpkin nose and pumpkin stalk.

1 Dust the workboard and knead the paste until smooth.

2 Flatten the base while gently pinching the top of the paste.

3 Shape the paste by hand to get a flat base, with four triangular sides, laying one side on the work surface at a time.

CUBOID

This basic shape can be made into a crocodile head and potion bottles.

1 Dust the workboard and knead the paste until smooth.

2 Flatten the paste on four sides to create a rough rectangular shape.

3 Pinch each corner into a sharp point.

4 To avoid leaving fingermarks, use two cake smoothers to flatten two surfaces at a time.

WEDGE

A piece of cheese or a lion's nose can be made from a wedge shape.

1 Dust the workboard and knead the paste until smooth.

2 Use your fingers to shape the paste into a triangle.

3 Flatten the shape against the workboard, using the cake smoother to assist so fingermarks are not left.

4 Move the wedge around so each surface is flattened.

5 Pinch the edges if they are not sufficiently defined, then flatten again.

DONUT

Donut shapes can be built up to create the body of a caterpillar, for example.

1 Dust the workboard and knead the paste until smooth.

2 Dust one palm with cornstarch and roll the paste in your palms to form a ball.

3 Flatten the ball slightly, then start thinning out the center of the ball with your index fingers. Continue thinning the center until it disappears and leaves a hole. Use the ball tool to neaten the hole.

HEART

A heart shape forms the basis for a rabbit head or bows.

1 Dust the workboard and knead the paste until smooth.

2 Dust one palm with cornstarch and roll the paste in the palm of your hands to form a ball.

3 Roll the paste on the edge of your palm to shape into a rough teardrop.

4 Flatten the shape between your palms slightly.

5 Use the stitch embossing tool to indent the paste at the top of the heart. Flatten a little further to accentuate the shape.

6 Use a separate pad of paste to remove any fingermarks.

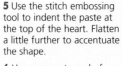

HEMISPHERE
This shape is good for frog eyes.

1 Dust the workboard and knead the paste until smooth.

2 Dust one palm with cornstarch and roll the paste in the palm of your hands to form a ball.

3 Using a sharp exacto knife, cut the ball in half, first by scoring around the center of the ball, then deepening the scoring carefully until cut fully through. Flatten the base.

EGG
An egg shape makes a good body for animals such as the pig on page 114.

1 Dust the workboard and knead the paste until smooth.

2 Dust one palm with cornstarch and roll the paste in the palm of your hands to form a ball.

3 Elongate one end of the shape in your palms to create an egg shape.

SAUSAGE
Arms and legs all start out as a sausage shape, so this is a very useful shape.

1 Dust the workboard and knead the paste until smooth.

2 Roll the paste on the workboard until a sausage shape forms. Alternatively, use a cake smoother.

CYLINDER
This shape makes good legs for animals, like the elephant on page 92.

1 Dust the workboard and knead the paste until smooth.

2 Use your fingers to roll the paste on the workboard into a sausage shape, then neaten using two cake smoothers.

3 Flatten each end of the cylinder using a cake smoother.

making basic figures

Making basic figures is easy when you know how. The male and female forms are composed of the same basic shapes, but there are differences between features, such as hair length, torso shape and height.

Choosing Your Medium

Your choice of medium will be decided by the way you want your figure to look, or your ability. If you are making figures that require detailed features, or that are wearing garments with fine or delicate frills, then flower paste is the most suitable medium (see pages 40–41). If you are a beginner, or detailing your figure is not important, then use gum paste or marzipan. Gum paste is particularly good as it allows beginners to mold again and again until the right shape is achieved. The bride and groom below were made using both gum paste and flower paste, and the boy and girl on the opposite page were made using only gum paste.

Figure Modeling Tools

Figures can be modeled completely by hand, with extra features, folds and creases made with the aid of simple modeling tools. Beginners may prefer to use a figure mold (available in most

cake decorating stores), but remember to prepare the paste so that it is malleable and free from cracks, and to dust the mold with cornstarch to ensure the paste doesn't stick. There are also molds available for individual parts of the figure—this allows you to create more lifelike facial features, and hands with neat fingers—although you can do this by hand, too, with a little patience!

Flower paste can be rolled out very thinly, which means it is ideal for making detailed models or delicate flowers, like the rose feature on this bride's dress.

You can support
drying limbs with a
piece of rolled-up
paper towel inserted
gently underneath
the limb.

Starting to Model Your Figure

Beginners should start by rolling basic shapes to
create the figure. Don't worry about capturing
the fingers on the hands or about getting the
figure to stand up. Start simple. You may find it
useful to work from the cake, sitting your figures
on the edge of the cake and building upward
from the legs and feet—as the sequence over
the page demonstrates.

Tools

- Gum paste
- Colorings
- Edible glue or
  water
- Shortening
- Paintbrush
- Dried spaghetti or
  sugar sticks
- Paper towel
- Piping tube

- Toothpicks
- Ball tool
- Exacto knife
- Extruder
- Palette knife
- Flower veining
  tool

Gum paste is malleable,
sturdy and easy to mold,
which makes it perfect for
the construction of basic
figures like these.

Making the Boy

The basic boy figure is clean and tidy; an excellent figure for a beginner to try. Change the color of his pants and shirt if you like.

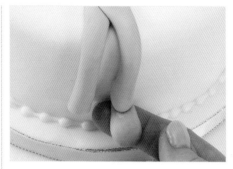

1 Roll out some paste to make two long, slim sausages. Bend them at the knee and lay over the curve of your cake.

Squash the tops together onto the cake and secure with water or a little edible glue.

2 Use different colored paste to make two shoes: shape balls into teardrop shapes and

secure to the bottom of the legs with edible glue or water. Support until dry.

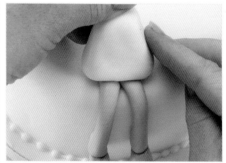

3 Using plain white gum paste—reserve about ½ oz. (15 g) for

the arms—make the body from a triangular shape with soft edges.

4 Sit the body on top of the legs, securing with edible glue, and support from behind until dry. If you wish you can add a

piece of dried spaghetti (or a sugar stick) through the body into the legs to add support to your figure.

See also
Working with Gum Paste, pages 60–63 > Essential Shapes, pages 64–67 > Working with Color, pages 54–59

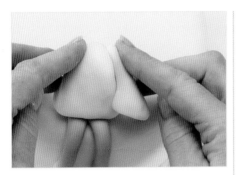

5 Divide the remaining paste in half and shape into two cones, then soften the edges. Secure to the shoulder area of the body using edible glue. Support with a little rolled-up paper towel until dry.

6 Shape an oval, slightly more pointed at one end (chin) and more rounded at the top (forehead).

7 Using the tip of a piping tube, indent the paste to mark where the two eyes will be, and use the wide end of the piping tube to indent a mouth.

8 Dampen the face where the nose is going and attach a nose using a toothpick and a pinch of flesh-colored paste. Do the same for the eyes in a color of your choice.

Essential Notes

> If you are working slowly, keep your paste wrapped in plastic wrap or a bag to ensure it doesn't dry out.

> If you are stuggling to keep your figure upright, use a strand of dried spaghetti to support it.

9 Make two tiny ears out of flesh-colored paste, indenting the paste using the ball tool. Attach them to the side of the head using edible glue.

10 Shape hands from the flesh-colored paste. First shape the paste into a teardrop, then use an exacto knife to cut five digits. Use a toothpick to give shape to the fingers.

11 Lastly, extrude orange paste through the extruder to create a neat hairstyle for your figure. Use the palette knife to gently position the hair in place on top of the head and attach using edible glue.

Essential Notes

> Changing the dial on your extruder will create different types of hairstyle.

> Always work from the body part that has the most contact with the cake base to ensure your model is as stable as possible.

Making the Girl

The basic girl figure is very similar to the boy figure, but her body shape is different and her hair longer. Change the color of her dress if you like.

1 Shape the paste into a cone. Bend the top quarter at right angles to make the waist. Add creases using the bone tool.

2 Shape the bodice, giving the girl a bust and neck. Narrow at the base for the waist and attach to the skirt using dried spaghetti and edible glue.

3 Shape the head, mark the mouth and eyes, and shape and attach the nose (see Steps 6–8 on page 71). Fix the head to the bodice using a dried strand of spaghetti.

4 Shape arms and legs from the flesh-colored paste. Form a sausage, flatten one end, and then bend upward to form a hand or foot. Fix to the body using dried spaghetti or edible glue.

5 Mix shortening with the orange paste and extrude long lengths from the extruder. Fix to the head in the same way as you did the boy's hair (see Step 11 opposite).

texturing

Sometimes it isn't enough to leave paste smooth. Rolled fondant, marzipan and modeling chocolate can all be textured to enhance the cake design by adding depth, detail and reality to your creation. The chosen texturing technique must complement the design, and a number of methods can be used together. Over the next eight pages, we feature over 20 different texturing methods for you to incorporate into your own topper designs, but there are plenty more to be discovered.

Texturing Tools

The most useful sugarcraft tools for texturing are the flower veining tool, extruder and stitch embossing tool (see pages 20–23); however, tools for texturing don't have to be professionally produced. Many household items will create a flawless texture, just right for the perfect design. Remember that items used for texturing must be properly cleaned and wiped with alcohol to remove any remnants of grease or other contaminants.

Folded fabric
Use the flower veining tool to indent deep and shallow lines to create the appearance of wrapped or folded fabric.

Patterned fabric
Paste can be patterned using embossers while it is still soft. Take care when positioning the paste not to press on the embossed section.

Facial features
To texture a face with facial features such as nose, mouth or eyes, use the flower veining tool.

Hair
Long, free strands of paste have been extruded through the extruder to give two large, full bunches, positioned on either side of the face. The back of the head has hair too, but the strands are pulled together. The bangs have been made using the same technique, but the hair has been cut short and attached randomly.

Joints
Paste is often indented at the elbows using the flower veining tool to add creases in clothes, naturally seen when the arms are bent.

Chiffon
This dress has been given a chiffon effect by using a textured rolling pin, rolled over soft paste before trimming and applying. Extra creases have been added using the flower veining tool.

Frills
The paste has been stretched and thinned along one edge using a round toothpick, then frilled further and creased and folded using the flower veining tool. The frill has been attached to the bottom of the dress and the stitch embossing tool used to emboss a stitching line around the skirt.

See also
Working with Color, pages 54–59 > Working with Gum Paste, pages 60–63 > Essential Shapes, pages 64–67

Tools

- Gum paste softened with shortening (see pages 40–41)
- Flower veining tool
- Edible glue
- Paintbrush

THICK HAIR
Pinch off small pieces of softened paste and roll them into long or short teardrops. Draw the flower veining tool along the teardrop to texture it. Attach with edible glue.

Tools

- Gum paste
- Flower veining tool
- Edible glue
- Paintbrush

FUR
Score the paste with the flower veining tool in the same direction, but starting at different levels. Roll small balls of the scored paste into teardrops. Draw the flower veining tool along each teardrop to make a tufts. Attach with edible glue.

Tools

- Gum paste softened with shortening (see pages 40–41)
- Extruder with multihole disk
- Knife
- Edible glue
- Paintbrush

THIN HAIR
Extrude the paste through the extruder. Scrape the paste off the extruder with the knife and attach to the figure using edible glue.

Tools

- Gum or flower paste
- Rolling pin
- Pizza wheel, exacto knife or cutter
- Foam pad
- Toothpick

PLEATS
Roll the paste and cut out the required shape. Place the paste on the foam pad with the edge to be frilled at the edge of the pad. Roll the toothpick back and forth over the paste, thinning and stretching it.

Tools

- Gum paste softened with shortening (see page 40–41)
- Flower veining tool

FOLDS IN FABRIC
Use the pointed end of the flower veining tool to indent the still-soft paste to form creases. Try to create many small creases rather than large, unnatural ones, but make some creases deeper than others.

Tools

- Rolled fondant
- Sieve
- Palette knife
- Edible glue
- Paintbrush

SHORT GRASS
Knead the rolled fondant until it is soft and warm. Push small balls of paste through the sieve. Scrape the paste off the sieve using a palette knife. Secure in place with edible glue.

Tools

- Rolled fondant
- Grater
- Sharp knife
- Edible glue
- Paintbrush

GRAVEL / SOIL
Finely grate the rolled fondant and allow it to dry, then finely chop with the sharp knife. Secure the soil in place using edible glue.

Tools

- Rolled fondant
- Flower veining tool
- Edible glue
- Paintbrush

LONG GRASS
Roll small balls of rolled fondant into teardrop shapes. Draw the flower veining tool down the length of each teardrop, and slightly curl over the tops of the tall ones. Group several teardrops together and secure with edible glue.

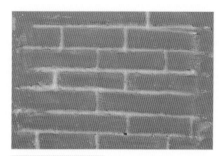

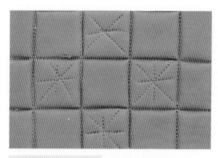

Tools

- Gum paste (colored to preferred shade)
- Ruler
- Flower veining tool
- Terra cotta dusting powder
- Paintbrush
- Piping bag and tube (No.1)
- Royal icing (colored to preferred shade)

BRICKWORK

Mark straight lines in the gum paste, using the edge of a ruler. Use the flower veining tool to emboss right-angled lines, and to make sure all the lines are defined. Dust the brickwork with a terra cotta dusting powder to add depth. Pipe royal icing into the embossed lines for the mortar, and use your finger to wipe off any excess.

Tools

- Gum paste
- Rolling pin
- Small square cutter
- Edible glue
- Paintbrushes
- Stitch embossing tool
- Dusting powders
- Vodka

PATCHWORK

Roll out the paste and use the square cutter to cut out squares. Thinly roll out some more paste to form a base. Use edible glue to fix the cutout squares closely together on the base. Run the stitch embossing tool between each square. Paint the squares different colors, following the method on page 59.

Tools

- Gum paste
- Textured rolling pin

GRILLE

Texture the paste by rolling the textured rolling pin carefully in one direction. Turn the rolling pin through 90 degrees and roll carefully again.

Tools

- Gum paste
- Flower veining tool or shaped cutters

DECORATIVE PATTERNS

Emboss freehand patterns into paste using the flower veining tool or shaped cutters.

Tools

- Gum paste
- Textured mat
- Cornstarch pad (for dusting)
- Rolling pin

CRATERED EFFECT

This effect is achieved using a textured mat, which is available in all sorts of patterns. Dust the mat lightly with cornstarch. Place the pattern side face down on soft paste. Evenly roll over the back of the mat with the rolling pin. Lift the mat away, leaving the textured paste behind.

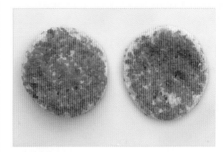

Tools

- Gum paste
- Toothpick
- Paintbrush
- Edible glue
- Pollen powder or semolina and dusting powder

POLLEN EFFECT

Prick the paste with the toothpick multiple times. Use the paintbrush to lightly paint the paste with edible glue. Sprinkle with pollen powder or semolina mixed with dusting powder to create a pollen effect suitable for the center of a flower.

Tools

- Gum paste
- Toothpick
- Stipple brush
- Orange paint

CITRUS PEEL

Prick the soft paste with the toothpick multiple times, very close together. Use a stipple brush loaded with orange paint to achieve great results.

Tools

- Gum paste leaves, still soft
- Foam pad
- Flower veining tool

VEINED LEAF

Place a paste leaf on the foam pad and draw the flower veining tool along it, creating veins on the leaf. Leaves can also be veined using a specific leaf veiner, but this can be expensive.

Tools

- Gum paste
- Textured rolling pin

STIPPLED EFFECT

Gently roll the textured pin over still-soft paste, keeping the pressure constant. You can create a variety of different textures with a textured rolling pin, so experiment.

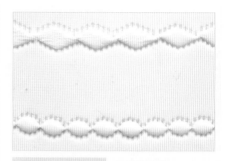

Tools

- Gum paste
- Crimpers

EMBOSSED EFFECT

This effect is created using crimpers. First make sure the crimpers are clean and dry. Squeeze the crimper teeth together, pinching the paste into a pattern.

Tools

- Gum paste
- Quilting wheel

LINEWORK

This effect is created using the quilting wheel. Quilting wheels can be bought in various different sizes to give different effects. Just roll the tool along the paste to create easy linework.

Tools

- Royal icing (colored to preferred shade)
- Boiled and cooled water
- Piping gel (see page 43)
- Paintbrushes

WATER

Soften the royal icing with the water or piping gel to achieve a suitable consistency for painting. Paint the softened icing onto dry paste or a dried topper, creating waves. Leave to dry. Paint the whole design with piping gel.

Tools	MOSS
• Royal icing (colored to preferred shade) • Flat-ended paintbrush or stencil brush	To cover a gum paste topper with a moss texture, use a flat-ended paintbrush to stipple colored royal icing onto the paste.

Tools	ROAD SURFACES
• Gum paste • Cheesecloth • Rolling pin • Knife • Edible glue • Paintbrush	Place cheesecloth over soft paste and roll with the rolling pin to emboss. For a gravel effect, use the knife to chop up small pieces of soft paste until they are fine and grainy. Glue in place with edible glue.

Tools	FEATHERS
• Royal icing • Gum paste • Paintbrush • Flower veining tool	Paint royal icing over the dried paste using a paintbrush. Draw the flower veining tool across the still-soft icing, and continue texturing the feathers in the icing until it starts to set.

Tools	LEATHER
• Gum paste • Luster dust	For a leather effect, polish luster dust into the paste using a piece of excess paste.

making templates

The ability to make your own template is invaluable when designing cakes. For example, an element of a design that would be too difficult to cut freehand can be cut with the help of a card template.

Tools

- Template shape
- Tracing paper
- Pencil
- Ruler
- Template card (such as that used for a cake box)
- Scissors
- Workboard
- Cornstarch pad (for dusting)
- Gum paste
- Rolling pin

Printed Templates
There are specific templates in this book that relate directly to the toppers in the directory, which you will need to enlarge in size. You will find these at the back of the book on pages 250–251. Alternatively, you may find a pattern in a magazine or on the Internet that you want to turn into an embossing pattern, or you may be making up a model of your own and are not sure what size of dress or bodice is required, in which case a template can be made, shaped to fit the model and then used to cut out the required feature in paste.

How To Use a Template
For patterns that require enlarging, the simplest method is to use a photocopier and enlarge to the size required. If a photocopier is not to hand, either enlarge by hand using squared paper or, if you think you have the eye for it, work freehand.

See also
Topper Directory, pages 86–249 > Templates, pages 250–251

Enlarging a Template

1 Lay tracing paper over your template shape and use a pencil to trace around the shape.

2 Decide how much larger you would like the pattern to be, for example, 1½ in. (4 cm) larger all around. Using the ruler, measure this distance away from the shape at various points around the motif, leaving a dot each time.

3 When you have gone all the way around the shape, join the dots and smooth out the lines.

4 Trace the enlarged motif onto template card and cut out. You now have your template. Dust the workboard and roll out the gum paste. Dust the paste again and position the template on top.

Cutting Paste From Templates

Templates are especially useful if you are using letters or numbers on your cake. Letters and numbers on a cake need to be executed well, as they are often very fiddly to make. While molds and cutters for letters and numbers are available, they are not as versatile as cutting your own in a style to match your cake. Think about the font you want to use, since you do not want the elements to be too small or simply too complicated to cut out.

Selecting Materials

The best paste to use for letters and numbers is flower paste, because it is a strong paste that dries hard, so the letters can stand upright on their own. Follow the sequence opposite to create neat and shapely letters starting from a template. Once complete and dry, the letters and numbers can be painted or dusted to add depth and interest. Once you are skilled at piping, they can be further illuminated with piped patterns or dots.

Tools

- Template card, pencil and scissors
- Flower paste
- Workboard
- Cornstarch pad for dusting
- Rolling pin
- Spacers
- Exacto knife or Kemper knife
- Wooden block or cake drum
- Emery board

Have fun cutting out different fonts, from simple, traditional shapes to more elaborate, playful ones. Try capital and lowercase letters. Alternatively, extrude paste from an extruder and then follow a line template of your favorite font.

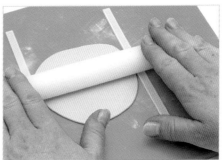

1 Cut out card templates of the letters or numbers you require, following the technique on page 83.

2 Roll out sufficient paste for one letter at a time, using spacers to ensure a uniform depth that can be repeated for each letter. Lightly dust the paste so the template will not stick to it, then place the template on the paste.

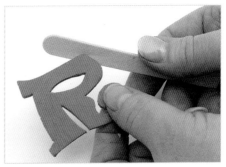

3 Carefully score around the template using the exacto knife or Kemper knife, then remove it. Use the exacto knife to carefully cut out the letter following the scored lines. Let the cutout paste dry on a cake drum dusted with cornstarch to prevent sticking.

4 If the edges of the letter are a little ragged, don't worry; wait until the letter is dry then use the emery board to lightly file away any rough edges.

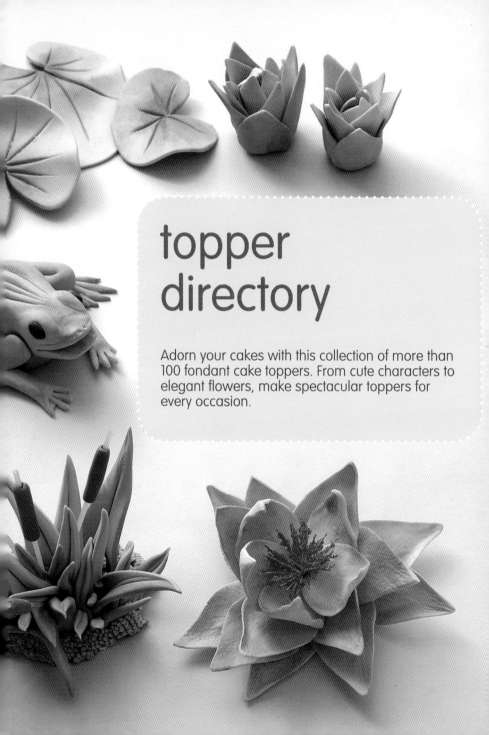

topper
directory

Adorn your cakes with this collection of more than 100 fondant cake toppers. From cute characters to elegant flowers, make spectacular toppers for every occasion.

lion

A very friendly lion, in a thoughtful pose.

Materials	Tools	Colors Used
• Gum paste • Colorings • Cornstarch (for dusting) • Dried spaghetti strands • Edible glue • Shortening	• Workboard • Flower veining tool • Paintbrush • Ball tool • Extruder with multihole disk	7½ oz. (210 g) ½ oz. (15 g) 1 oz. (30 g) Pinch Pinch

See also
Working with Color, pages 54–59 > Working with Gum Paste, pages 60–63 > Texturing, pages 74–81

4 Use 2 oz. (60 g) of gold paste for the head. Shape into a teardrop and attach to the body with the point of the teardrop uppermost. Use the flower veining tool to suggest whiskers and cheeks. Allow the head to rest on top of the front paws.

5 Make a nose using ½ oz. (15 g) of brown paste and attach it at the top of the cheeks. Use the small end of the ball tool to indent the nostrils. Divide a pinch of white paste into two balls and flatten to make two eyeballs. Do the same with a pinch of black for the pupils. Attach using edible glue.

3 Use ½ oz. (15 g) of gold paste for each of the front legs. Shape into a bone shape with the center narrower than the ends and one end bigger than the other. Attach the largest end to the body, in line with the neck, using edible glue. Cross one paw over the top of the other. Using the flower veining tool, indent the ends of the paws.

6 Mix shortening with the orange paste to soften it. Extrude the paste through the extruder at different lengths and attach around the head and face for the mane, saving a little for the tuft of the tail. Attach with edible glue.

2 Use ½ oz. (15 g) of gold paste for each of the back legs. Shape each into a teardrop, lengthen the point, then, using the flower veining tool, bend the fatter part of the leg over. Attach each leg to the side of the body at the back using edible glue, and indent the paws using the flower veining tool.

7 Roll the remaining gold paste into a sausage for the tail. Drape it around the body and tuck under the bottom a little.

1 Take 3 oz. (90 g) of gold paste and shape it into an egg shape for the body. Push three strands of spaghetti into the front and angle them backward in preparation for the head.

2 crocodile

This crocodile looks like he is after a tasty treat.

Materials

- Gum paste
- Colorings
- Cornstarch (for dusting)
- Edible glue

Tools

- Workboard
- Flower veining tool
- Ball tool
- Bone tool
- Paper towel
- Exacto knife
- Paintbrush

Colors Used

- 4½ oz. (130 g)
- 1 oz. (30 g)
- 1 oz. (30 g)
- Pinch

See also
Working with Color, pages 54–59 > Working with Gum Paste, pages 60–63 > Essential Shapes, pages 64–67

2 Model the head from 3 oz. (90 g) of green paste. Shape it into a rectangle and smooth off the corners. Smooth the large end of the ball tool down the center of the head, allowing each side to bulge out to make the eye sockets, then the nostrils.

3 Indent the eye sockets and nostrils using the bone tool. Use your fingers to accentuate the eye section, less so around the nose. Place on top of the lower jaw, using a rolled paper towel to keep the mouth open slightly while it dries.

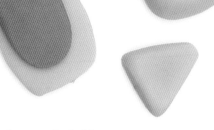

1 Using 1 oz. (30 g) of green paste, model the jawbone by shaping into a rectangle. Use the flower veining tool to indent the center of the jaw in preparation for the tongue. Shape the pink paste into a tongue, making it thin at the front and bulging at the back. Place on top of the jawbone.

4 Shape ½ oz (15 g) of green paste into two triangles to make two humps rising from the water.

6 Use the remnants of white paste for the eyeballs and a pinch of black paste to finish off the eyes and eyebrows.

5 Cut the teeth from the white paste using the exacto knife. Attach to the mouth with edible glue.

elephant

These playful elephants are fun to make in whatever pose you choose.
They can be wrapped around letters for a christening cake or numbers for
a birthday cake.

Materials

- Gum paste
- Colorings
- Cornstarch (for dusting)
- Dried spaghetti strand
- Edible lusters: silver, burgundy
- Edible glue

Tools

- Workboard
- Flower veining tool
- Kemper knife
- Paintbrushes

Colors Used

- 5¼ oz. (147 g)
- Pinch
- Pinch
- Pinch

See also

Working with Color, pages 54–59 > Working with Gum Paste, pages 60–63 > Essential Shapes, pages 64–67

3 Add a ruffled hairstyle, blush the cheeks with luster, and add black dots for eyes.

2 Shape the head and trunk from ¾ oz. (20 g) of gray. Make a smooth ball, then form a teardrop for the trunk. Indent eye sockets using the flower veining tool. Slit the end of the trunk open with the Kemper knife. Open the slit up using the flower veining tool and indent within the slit to make nostrils. Curl the trunk and mark creases on the curve.

4 Make the ears from ½ oz. (15 g) each of gray, formed into kidney shapes— flattened and widened at the top. Make white ear inserts, ensuring they are thinner and smaller than the ears. Secure with edible glue.

5 Shape two front legs from ½ oz. (15 g) each of gray. Make the base quite flat and curve to create "elbows." Use the flower veining tool to crease around the elbows.

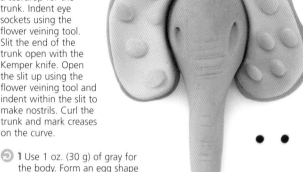

1 Use 1 oz. (30 g) of gray for the body. Form an egg shape with a flat base. Place a strand of spaghetti through the neck to support the head.

8 Make toenails using three tiny balls of pale blue. Secure together with edible glue, flatten a little, and then cut off one side of the balls to give a flat edge. Attach to the legs with edible glue.

7 Shape the back legs in the same way as the front, but make the legs a little thinner and accentuate the feet.

6 Roll about ½ oz. (15 g) of gray to create the tail. Cut the ends using the Kemper knife to form a fan effect. Attach to the body with edible glue.

4 dinosaur

What about this cute red dinosaur on a birthday cake? He is not too difficult to make and would delight any child.

Materials	Tools
• Gum paste	• Workboard
• Colorings	• Rolling pin
• Cornstarch (for dusting)	• Exacto knife
	• Flower veining tool
• Dried spaghetti strands	• Paintbrush
	• Piping tube
• Edible glue	• Pizza wheel
• ¼ in. (5 mm) width stem tape	• Textured rolling pin
	• Former

Colors Used

● 8 oz. (225 g)
○ Pinch
● Pinch
● 1 oz. (30 g)

See also
Working with Color, pages 54–59 > Working with Gum Paste, pages 60–63 > Essential Shapes, pages 64–67

4 Flatten ¼ oz. (7 g) of red paste with your fingers to make a small pad. Place the pad on the chest section of the dinosaur to build up the chest and support the neck. Use the flower veining tool to squash the paste onto the body and add in deep and shallow creases.

5 Shape the head from ¾ oz. (20 g) of red paste formed into a rectangle that is bigger at one end. At the narrow end of the head, use the broad edge of the piping tube to indent the mouth. Use the flower veining tool to indent the nostrils and add creases around the nose and eyes.

6 Make eyes from pinches of white paste shaped into teardrops. Attach using edible glue. Attach black pupils in the same way.

7 Shape ⅛ oz. (3.5 g) of red paste into teardrops for the ears. Draw the flower veining tool across the shape to add texture, and fix in place with edible glue.

3 Cut off 2 in. (5 cm) of red paste from the neck, as shown. This is the section that will be inserted into the dinosaur's body. Insert the neck into the body 1 in. (2.5 cm) in from the end.

8 Shape the two front legs from 1 oz. (30 g) of red paste. Make an oval, then use the flower veining tool to flatten one end and bend upward to form the foot. Indent twice to make toe effects and form creases around the ankle. Join to the body using edible glue. Form creases where the legs meet the body using the flower veining tool. Do the same with the back legs, but on a larger scale.

2 Take three spaghetti strands of about 6½ in. (16.5 cm) and tape them together with stem tape. Cover the strands with edible glue. Roll out ¾ oz. (20 g) of red paste thinly, then roll the strand package up in the paste until covered. Trim off excess paste with the exacto knife. This forms the dinosaur's neck.

9 Roll the green paste into a thin strip. Trim the edges using the pizza wheel. Use the textured rolling pin to texture, then wrap around the neck, draping it down the chest. To make tassels for the scarf, shape green paste into squares then score with the exacto knife—do not cut all the way through. Attach with edible glue.

10 With the remaining red paste, shape a long, thin cone shape for the tail. Use the flower veining tool to add texture. Attach to the body with edible glue. Use a former to support the tail in a curvy shape until dry.

1 Shape the body from 3 oz. (90 g) of red paste. Form into an oval shape with flattened ends.

5 cat

This delightful cat is a thoroughly pampered feline.

Materials	Tools	Colors used
• Gum paste	• Workboard	● 5 oz. (140 g)
• Colorings	• Flower veining tool	● ½ oz. (15 g)
• Cornstarch (for dusting)	• Exacto knife	○ 1½ oz. (45 g)
• Dried spaghetti strands	• Paintbrush	● 1 oz. (30 g)
• Edible glue	• Ball tool	
• White stamens		

See also
Working with Color, pages 54–59 > Working with Gum Paste, pages 60–63 > Texturing, pages 74–81

2 Use 1 oz. (30 g) of lilac paste to make the head. Roll it into a sausage shape first, then elongate either end to shape the "fur" on either side. Use the flower veining tool to add texture to these areas, shaping in an outward motion. Now do the facial features (see Steps 8–11 on page 98).

BODY

3 Use ½ oz. (15 g) of lilac paste for the front legs. Roll into a thin sausage, cut in half using the exacto knife and flatten one end. Use edible glue to attach the flattened end to the body below the neck. Bend the paw end out.

1 Take 2 oz. (60 g) of lilac paste and mold into a conical shape for the body, tapering as you work upward. Push a strand of dried spaghetti into the neck section and down through the body as support for the head, leaving ⅜ in. (1 cm) exposed.

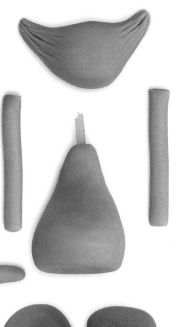

4 Make the white front chest using ½ oz. (15 g) of white paste, rolled out to flatten and textured with the flower veining tool to give a fur effect, then trimmed with the exacto knife. Use the glue to attach it to the neck area so it covers the top of the front legs.

7 Roll the remainder of the lilac paste out into a long teardrop to make the tail. Tuck it slightly under the cat at the back.

5 Shape each back leg from ½ oz. (15 g) of lilac paste and attach with edible glue to either side of the back.

6 Make four tiny paws from four little balls of white paste. Sit them in place and indent the paw shape using the flower veining tool.

Continued over the page ➡

FACIAL FEATURES

8 Turn to page 97, Step 2, for instructions on how to create the head.

11 Shape two teardrop eyes using pinches of white and black paste. Attach to the face using edible glue. Make a tiny nose from black paste and secure it to the face between the cheeks using edible glue, then add black eyebrows.

10 Make the cheeks using 15 g (½ oz) of white paste shaped into two teardrop shapes, and attach to the face, partially covering the mouth. Prick with the pointed end of the flower veining tool, then insert the white stamen strands as whiskers, cutting the stamen ends off first.

9 Use the smaller end of the ball tool to indent the mouth, then use the flower veining tool to refine the shape and put a crease under the chin to accentuate the mouth a little more. Attach a tiny piece of pink paste for the tongue. When you have finished the facial features, attach the head to the body using edible glue.

ACCESSORIES

12 Make two bows from the remainder of the pink paste, a large one for around the neck and a small one for the top of the head. Attach the larger bow around the neck with the bow at the front.

13 Use pinches of lilac paste to make three tiny teardrops. Attach these to the top of the head using the flower veining tool. Attach the little bow to this sprout of hair.

6 duckling

This sweet topper is suitable for all sorts of celebrations, including a christening.

Materials	Tools
• Gum paste	• Workboard
• Colorings	• Bone tool
• Cornstarch (for dusting)	• Flower veining tool
• Edible glue	• Rolling pin
	• Template card, pencil and scissors
	• Exacto knife
	• Paintbrush

Colors Used

- ⬤ 6 oz. (170 g)
- ⬤ 1 oz. (30 g)
- ⬤ Pinch

See also
Working with Color, pages 54–59 > Working with Gum Paste, pages 60–63 > Texturing, pages 74–81

2 Roll out the remaining white paste, but not too thinly. Cut two wings from the paste. Using your fingers, soften the cut edges, then texture the wings using the flower veining tool. Attach a wing to each side of the body using edible glue on the front section of the wing only, leaving the back part free.

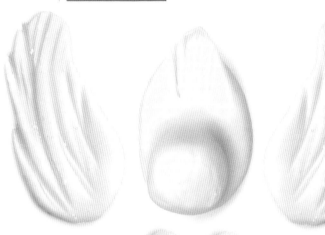

1 Shape the head and body from 4½ oz. (130 g) of white paste. Start with a ball shape. Elongate it to form a narrower section for the neck, leaving a rounded head. Use the bone tool to indent two eye sockets and build out the eyebrows a little. Shape the tail section, then use the flower veining tool to frill the tail and give the impression of feathers.

3 Shape two white balls for the eye sockets and indent them with the ball tool. Use a pinch of black paste to make two small balls for eyes, and attach the eyes to the sockets using edible glue.

4 Form a wedge shape for the beak from ¼ oz. (7 g) of orange paste. Slit the pointed end using the exacto knife. Shape the end of the beak.

5 Use ¾ oz. (20 g) of orange paste for the two feet. Start each foot by forming a triangle, soften the corners, then use the flower veining tool to indent the foot. Attach each foot to the body with edible glue, and support until dry.

7 mouse

This cute white mouse is easy to make in two main parts, although shaping the head and body from one piece can be difficult.

Materials

- Gum paste
- Cornstarch (for dusting)
- Dried spaghetti strands
- Edible glue
- 24 ga. silver wire
- Royal icing

Tools

- Workboard
- Flower veining tool
- Paintbrush
- Ball tool
- Bone tool
- Kemper knife

Colors Used

- 4 oz. (115 g)
- Pinch
- ½ oz. (15 g)
- 1½ oz. (45 g)

See also
Working with Color, pages 54–59 > Working with Gum Paste, pages 60–63 > Texturing, pages 74–81

3 Roll two eyes and a nose from the black paste and fix in place with edible glue.

4 Split the paste reserved in Step 2 into two balls for ears. Use the large end of the ball tool to shape hollow, thinning edges, leaving each ear thicker at the back. Attach to the head using small dabs of edible glue, then use the bone tool to gently rub the base of each ear onto the head so the join disappears.

2 Take 1 oz. (30 g) of white paste. Pinch off a little for both ears, then shape the remaining paste into a long teardrop for the head, with a flattened end for the nose. Use the ball tool to indent either side of the nose for eye sockets. Attach the head to the body, over the spaghetti strand, using edible glue to assist.

5 Shape the hands and feet from ½ oz. (15 g) of pink paste, ensuring the hands are smaller than the feet. Shape into a triangle, then flatten a broad section. Cut each element into four sections, trimming away the excess to make the fingers and toes. Attach to the body using edible glue.

1 Shape 2½ oz. (75 g) of white paste into a broad, squat ball. Use the flower veining tool to indent the shape of the back leg. Insert a spaghetti strand into the body as support for the head.

9 Cut 24 ga. silver wire into six strips, two long, two medium and two short. Curl each wire slightly at one end and insert the other end of each into the nose to create the whiskers.

8 Mix the royal icing so that it is soft but not runny, and use a paintbrush to apply it to the mouse to give a furry effect.

7 Use the remaining pink paste to shape a tail. Make a sausage, narrowing the end to a point. Slide under the body and leave to dry in a coiled position.

6 Shape yellow paste into a wedge and use the small end of the ball tool to make holes. Fix the cheese under the nose with edible glue.

8 swan

A most beautiful and elegant swan, and yet so easy to make.

Materials

- Gum paste
- Cornstarch (for dusting)
- 22 ga. wire
- Edible glue
- Gum paste powder
- Royal icing
- Colorings, including poinsettia and black
- Silver snowflake dusting powder

Tools

- Workboard
- Flower veining tool
- Paper towels
- Rolling pin
- Template card, pencil and scissors (optional)
- Exacto knife
- Paintbrushes

Colors Used

- 2¾ oz. (82 g)

See also
Working with Color, pages 54–59 > Texturing, pages 74–81 > Templates, pages 250–251

2 For the body, shape 1½ oz. (45 g) of white paste into a teardrop. Flatten the pointed end to fan out the tail. Use the flower veining tool to texture the tail feathers. Raise this section up and away from the work surface and support until dry, if necessary, on a paper towel.

3 Work a small amount of gum paste powder into 1 oz. (30 g) of white paste to stiffen it. Roll the paste out thickly and use the template (see page 250) and exacto knife to cut out two wings. Stand the wings upright and curve them around the swan's body. Curve the feathers slightly inward to make a more elegant shape. Leave to dry.

4 Use a paintbrush to apply royal icing to the wings to give a feathery effect. Leave upright to dry.

1 For the neck, mold ¼ oz. (7 g) of white paste into a sausage shape that is thin at one end and fatter at the other. Push 22 ga. wire through the center of the sausage to support the neck. Thin and flatten the thinner end of the sausage, leaving a bulge just in front of the eyes. Curve the neck. Flatten the fatter end to aid attachment to the body. Leave to dry.

5 Use royal icing to fix all the pieces together, and support until dry.

7 Using a clean, dry paintbrush, dust the swan with silver snowflake dusting powder to add sparkle.

6 Apply poinsettia coloring to the beak with a paintbrush and allow to dry. Outline in black coloring.

9 frog

This cheerful model teams well with the water lily, bulrushes and lily pads (see pages 208–209). You could also make the top of your cake look like a lily pad and place your frog on top.

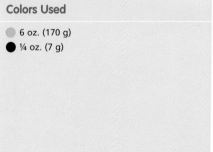

Materials

- Gum paste
- Colorings
- Cornstarch (for dusting)
- Edible glue
- Daffodil and fern green dusting powders

Tools

- Workboard
- Bone tool
- Exacto knife
- Flower veining tool
- Foam pad
- Paintbrushes

Colors Used

- 6 oz. (170 g)
- ¼ oz. (7 g)

See also
Working with Color, pages 54–59 > Working with Gum Paste, pages 60–63 > Texturing, pages 74–81

3 Use the flower veining tool to indent the very front of the top lip with two dots for nostrils. Use the flower veining tool to texture the face, drawing the tool from the eye to the nostrils. Make the eyes with the black paste and attach.

4 Curve the head up slightly and support with a foam pad until dry.

5 Make back legs using 2 oz. (60 g) of green paste. Shape the paste into a long sausage that is broad at one end, getting thinner. Flatten the thinner end to make the foot. Bend the leg from the broad end to make the first joint, and use the flower veining tool to neaten the crease. Make the bend tight. Do the same for the second joint.

6 Use the exacto knife to cut toes, but remember not to cut too deeply, ensuring you keep a webbed look. Use the flower veining tool to accentuate the webbed toes by drawing the tool up toward the ankle. Trim the toes with the exacto knife.

7 Attach the back legs to the body by flattening ⅛ in. (5 mm) of the broad end of each leg and tucking this under the frog. Secure with edible glue.

2 Cut the mouth using the exacto knife, then open and deepen it. Use the flower veining tool to soften the cut, shaping the point.

1 Mold 3 oz. (90 g) of green paste into an egg shape, the broader end being the back of the frog. Shape the head end further to make the face and mouth more pointed. Use the bone tool to indent the eyes, pulling the paste to make the area around the eyes bulge upward.

9 Use a paintbrush to apply dusting powders in varying quantities along the body and back to achieve a change in color.

8 Shape the front legs in the same way as the back but using 1 oz. (30 g) of green paste and making these slightly shorter and with only one joint. When attaching to the body, the joints jut outward and the feet point in slightly. Secure as before.

10 butterfly

A fabulous butterfly that is made in two parts. Both of the wings are worked in the same way, only as mirror images of each other.

Materials	Tools	Colors Used
• Gum paste • Colorings • Cornstarch (for dusting) • Gum paste powder • Shortening • Edible glue • Royal icing • 24 ga. silver wire • Dusting powders of your choice	• Template card, pencil and scissors • Workboard • Exacto knife • Rolling pin • Various cutters, such as paisley cutters, curves and coils • Piping tube No. 1 • Small square cake drum • Extruder with single-hole disk • Foam pads • Paintbrush	○ 3 oz. (90 g) ● 1 oz. (30 g)

See also
Working with Color, pages 54–59 > Making Templates, pages 82–84 > Templates, pages 250–251

4 Use the tip of the piping tube and cutters to emboss dots, curves and coils, and place the paste wing on a dusted cake drum to dry.

5 Follow Steps 1–4 to make the second wing, remembering to work it as a mirror image of the first wing.

6 While the wings are drying, mix the offcuts of white paste with shortening and use the extruder to extrude a string of paste. Attach the string around the outside of each wing using edible glue. Use the exacto knife to neaten. Leave to dry.

3 Use the relevant cutters to cut out the various shapes that were planned in Step 1, taking care to keep away from the edges of the paste.

2 Roll out 1½ oz. (45 g) of white paste. Place the wing template on the paste and cut around it with the exacto knife. Add gum paste powder to strengthen.

1 Use scissors to cut out the butterfly wing template (see page 250). Plan and mark out your preferred pattern of cutout and embossed shapes.

9 Cut two lengths of wire, curl the ends and add to the head. Apply pink dusting powders to the head, body and edges of the model.

8 Make a small ball of white paste for the head and shape the body into a long teardrop, elongating the point and curling it up. Use royal icing to fix between the two wings.

7 Roll out the pink paste and use edible glue to attach it to the underside of the wings to fill in the cut out sections. Use foam pads to raise up the outer edges.

11 ladybug

This simple ladybug is teamed with an unwired daisy here. If you'd like to make the flower base, turn to page 123.

Materials	Tools	Colors Used
• Gum paste	• Workboard	🔴 2 oz. (60 g)
• Colorings	• Kemper knife	⚫ 1 oz. (30 g)
• Cornstarch (for dusting)	• Flower veining tool	⚪ Pinch
• Edible glue	• Piping tube	
	• Paintbrush	

See also
Working with Color, pages 54–59 > Making Templates, pages 82–84 > Templates, pages 250–251

3 Make two antennae from pinches of black paste. Roll the paste in your hand to lengthen and thin the ends. Secure to the head using edible glue.

4 Make two eyeballs with small balls of white and then black paste.

2 Make the head from ¾ oz. (20 g) of black paste. Indent a mouth using the large end of the piping tube.

5 Use the remaining black paste to make the black dots on the body, fixed in place with edible glue.

1 Shape the red paste into an oval for the body. Slice the oval in half, but not all the way through, using the Kemper knife. Use the flower veining tool to soften the slit.

12 caterpillar

The caterpillar is a quick and easy topper to make. Use the colors shown here, or create your own color scheme.

Place a paper towel here until dry.

1 Shape the head from 1 oz. (30 g) of green paste.

2 Add eyes using pinches of white and black paste. Form the nose out of a pinch of green paste.

3 Fashion the mouth using the edge of the piping tube.

4 Make hair by extruding green paste mixed with shortening through the extruder to give strands of paste.

Secure these to the head using edible glue.

5 Make different sizes of balls with the remaining pastes for the caterpillar's body. Choose different colors to sit next to each

other, following an undulating pattern, and fix together with edible glue.

6 When the body is dry, stand the caterpillar up and attach head to body with edible glue.

Materials	Tools	Colors Used	
• Gum paste	• Workboard	⬤	2 oz. (60 g)
• Colorings	• Piping tube	⬤	½ oz. (15 g)
• Cornstarch (for dusting)	• Extruder with multihole disk	⬤	1 oz. (30 g)
• Edible glue	• Paintbrush	⬤	1 oz. (30 g)
• Shortening	• Paper towel	⬤	½ oz. (15 g)
		⬤	½ oz. (15 g)
		⬤	½ oz. (15 g)
		⬤	Pinch

13 shark

Simple but effective, this topper is designed to look as if the shark is emerging from the cake.

Blue and white royal icing creates a watery scene.

1 Make the tail from 1 oz. (30 g) of gray paste. Use the flower veining tool to indent the tail.

2 Shape the body and head from 3 oz. (90 g) of gray paste. Model the shark's pointed nose. Use the exacto knife to cut the mouth. Use a paper towel to keep the mouth open. Score the nose with the flower veining tool.

3 Indent the eye sockets using the ball tool. Add the eyes.

4 Use the exacto knife to cut the teeth from the white paste.

5 Roll out the pink paste thickly and use it to line the mouth, then, while it is still damp, insert the teeth into the edge of the pink paste. Fix in place using edible glue.

6 Cover the shark with piping gel to give a watery effect.

Materials

- Gum paste
- Colorings
- Cornstarch (for dusting)
- Edible glue
- Piping gel

Tools

- Workboard
- Flower veining tool
- Exacto knife
- Paper towel
- Ball tool
- Paintbrush
- Rolling pin

Colors Used

- 4 oz. (115 g)
- Pinch
- ½ oz. (15 g)
- 1 oz. (30 g)

14 pig

A family of pigs is easy to make when you know how.

Add brown-colored royal icing to create mud splashes.

1 Use 2 oz. (60 g) of pale pink paste to make the body and shape 1 oz. (30 g) of pale pink paste into a cone shape for the head.

2 Roll 1 oz. (30 g) of pale pink into a sausage and cut into four equal pieces using the exacto knife. Push short strands of spaghetti through each one, protruding ¼ in. (5 mm). Secure all four legs together using edible glue, then place the body on top.

3 Push spaghetti strands through the front of the body as support for the head and press the head into place.

4 Make heart-shaped ears with mini heart inserts from a pinch of dark pink paste and secure to the head with edible glue. Make the snout from ½ oz. (15 g) of dark pink paste, indenting the nostrils with the ball tool. Use the flower veining tool to indent the mouth. Make two eyes using a pinch of black paste rolled into balls and attach with edible glue.

5 Roll a small remnant of pale pink paste in the palms of your hands to make a curly tail.

Materials	Tools
• Gum paste	• Workboard
• Colorings	• Exacto knife
• Cornstarch (for dusting)	• Paintbrush
• Dried spaghetti strands	• Ball tool
• Edible glue	• Flower veining tool

Colors Used

- 4½ oz. (130 g)
- 1 oz. (30 g)
- Pinch

15 sheep

Add a sheep or two to the pigs opposite to create a farm-themed cake.

1 Shape the body from 2½ oz. (75 g) of white paste, using the flower veining tool to texture and crease.

2 Roll a sausage shape from 1 oz. (30 g) of black paste and use the exacto knife to cut it into four equal lengths for the legs. Insert dried spaghetti strands into each, leaving ¼ in. (5 mm) protruding. Make feet using ¼ oz. (7 g) of black paste and attach to the base of the legs with edible glue. Stand the legs together and place the body on top, over the spaghetti.

3 Push spaghetti strands through the front of the body as support for the head. Shape 1 oz. (30 g) of black paste into an oval for the head and press it into place over the spaghetti.

4 Using remnants of black paste, make two eyes, a nose and two ears, and attach to the head with edible glue. Shape the mouth using the flower veining tool, then, using remnants of white paste, make a tuft for the top of the head. Texture, as for the body.

Materials	Tools	Colors Used
• Gum paste	• Workboard	○ 3 oz. (90 g)
• Colorings	• Flower veining	● 3 oz. (90 g)
• Cornstarch (for dusting)	tool	
• Dried spaghetti strands	• Exacto knife	
• Edible glue	• Paintbrush	

16 rose

This beautiful, delicate flower is easy to make and looks amazing, so there is no need to shy away from making the rose topper.

Materials

- Flower paste (alternatively, use modeling chocolate)
- Cornstarch (for dusting)
- Edible glue

Tools

- Workboard
- Toothpicks
- Rolling pin
- Rose petal cutter (medium)
- Foam pad
- Bone tool

Colors Used

● 2 oz. (60 g)

See also
Working with Color, pages 54–59 > Working with Gum Paste, pages 60–63 > Texturing, pages 74–81

4 Using edible glue to fix the petals, begin by attaching the first petal to the cone from Step 1 by one edge, then wrap it around the cone, but before you stick down the whole petal, start the second petal so they intertwine. Tease the petals once attached so they are slightly open.

3 For the first layer, use the rose petal cutter to cut out two petals. Place them on the foam pad and soften with the bone tool, then work around the curved edge of the petal with a toothpick, stretching the paste and frilling it.

2 Roll out the remaining flower paste. Cut out only the required petals for each layer, otherwise they will dry too quickly. In this instance, you will need two petals for the first layer, three for the second and five for the final layer.

5 For the second layer, cut three petals and follow the same instructions, intertwining all three. Tease the petals out further and curl them backward a little using a toothpick.

1 Using ¼ oz. (7 g) of flower paste, make a cone shape and impale it on the end of a round toothpick.

6 For the final layer, cut five petals and follow the instructions in Steps 4 and 5. Take the flower off the toothpick and place on a flat surface until dry.

wired daffodil

This is an elegant-looking flower that is easy to make with a little skill.

Materials

- Gum paste
- Colorings
- Cornstarch (for dusting)
- 24 ga. green wire
- Edible glue

Tools

- Workboard
- Daffodil trumpet veiner
- Toothpick
- Paintbrush
- Rolling pin
- Daffodil head cutter
- Foam pad
- Bone tool
- Flower veining tool
- Pizza wheel

Colors Used

1 oz. (30 g)
1 oz. (30 g)
1 oz. (30 g)

See also
Working with Color, pages 54–59 > Working with Gum Paste, pages 60–63 > Texturing, pages 74–81

3 Push a large ball of yellow paste into the trumpet veiner and use the end of a toothpick to push the paste against the sides of the veiner. Use the toothpick to form a central hole in the trumpet.

4 Thread the trumpet down the wire, securing it around the ball at the end with edible glue. Keep the flower upside down until dry.

5 Roll out the white paste quite thinly, and use the head cutter to cut out one or two flower heads for the trumpet.

6 Place the flowers on the foam pad. Use the bone tool to soften them. Add texture and veins using the flower veining tool.

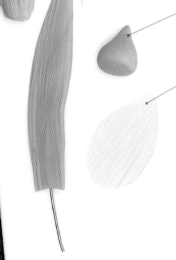

7 Make a seed pod from a pinch of green paste.

8 Thinly roll out the remaining white paste to make the dried bud case. Cut out a teardrop shape and texture using the flower veining tool.

2 Push a small ball of yellow paste down the wire. Make sure it covers the hook at the end.

1 Cut the wire to the desired length. Bend the wire over at one end to form a hook.

10 Roll out the remaining green paste and, using the pizza wheel, cut out elliptical-shaped leaves. Push a wire up the center of the leaf then soften the edges of the leaf on the foam pad using the bone tool. Use the flower veining tool to add veins and bend the leaf around the central vein.

9 Attach the flowers to the back of the trumpet by threading down the wire and securing with edible glue. Next, slide on the dried bud case and seed pod. Bend the wire at 90 degrees just behind the seed pod.

18 carnation

These cheerful carnations are very quick and easy to put together, and finish a birthday cake perfectly.

Materials	Tools
• Gum paste • Colorings • Cornstarch (for dusting) • Edible glue	• Workboard • Rolling pin • Carnation cutter • Foam pad • Toothpick • Paintbrush • Pizza wheel • Flower veining tool • Leaf cutter

Colors Used

● 2 oz. (60 g)
○ 2 oz. (60 g)
● 2 oz. (60 g)

See also
Working with Color, pages 54–59 > Working with Gum Paste, pages 60–63 > Texturing, pages 74–81

3 Apply edible glue to the center, almost all the way up to the frilled section, then apply around the folded shape, squeezing it so it is secure and shaping it into a circle.

2 Lay the carnation shapes on a foam pad and use a toothpick to frill the edges of the shapes. Fold the shape in half and secure in this position with edible glue, then fold again and secure in the same way.

4 Roll out the white paste very thinly. Use the pizza wheel to trim the rolled paste to a rectangle.

1 Thinly roll out the red paste. Use the carnation cutter to cut out three carnation shapes for each flower, but make one flower at a time, otherwise the paste will dry out.

8 Cut out two leaves using the leaf cutter and the remnants of green paste, rolled very thinly. Place the leaves on the green ball in preparation for the flowers to be added on top.

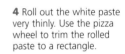

5 Make small sausages from ½ oz. (15 g) of green paste for the stems. Wrap the stems up by folding the white paste over, and secure with edible glue. Make a pinch where the bow will sit using the flower veining tool.

7 With ½ oz. (15 g) of green paste, cut out the bow and attach it to the bouquet at the point of the indentation made in Step 5.

6 Use another ¾ oz. (20 g) of green paste to make a ball shape at the top of the "stems"; this will be where the flowers are attached.

daisy

The daisy is a difficult cake topper because of its delicate petals. But persevere and you will achieve some excellent results.

Materials

- Gum paste (with added gumtex)
- Colorings
- Cornstarch (for dusting)
- 24 ga. green wire
- ¼ in. (5 mm) width stem tape
- Edible glue
- Leaf green dusting powder

Tools

- Workboard
- Rolling pin
- Daisy cutter
- Foam pad
- Bone tool
- Paintbrush
- Daisy center mold
- Petal blossom cutter
- Pizza wheel
- Flower veining tool

Colors Used

- 1½ oz. (45 g)
- ½ oz. (15 g)
- 2 oz. (60 g)

See also
Working with Color, pages 54–59 > Working with Gum Paste, pages 60–63 > Texturing, pages 74–81

3 Attach the shapes two together, with petals sitting side by side, using edible glue. Push a wire through the petals. Secure with edible glue and hang the flower upside down to dry.

4 Make the center of the flower using ¼ oz. (7 g) of yellow paste. Use a daisy center mold if you have one. Secure over the center of the petals using edible glue.

2 Roll out the white paste thinly and use the daisy cutter to cut out two daisy heads per flower, so six in total. Cut one at a time because the paste will dry quickly. Place a daisy shape on the foam pad and soften the edges of the petals using the bone tool. Set this to one side and cut and soften the second shape in the same way.

5 Roll out a small amount of green paste. Cut out a blossom shape. Soften on the foam pad using the bone tool, then thread up the wire behind the petals to form a sepal. Secure with edible glue.

6 Thickly roll out the green paste and use the pizza wheel to cut long oval leaf shapes. Push wire through the paste. Use the flower veining tool to texture the leaf, curving it slightly in or out.

7 Use the paintbrush to dust the surface of the leaves with the leaf green dusting powder to give realistic shades of color.

As a variation, make a wireless daisy head by shaping teardrops and adding them to the center piece to create petals.

1 Tape three 24 ga. wires of differing lengths with stem tape. Bend the top of the wire to make a flat coil.

20 maple leaf

A simple leaf design like the maple, placed elegantly in the center or at the edge of a cake, creates a sophisticated look.

Lightly dust the leaf edges to give a two-toned effect.

1 Roll out the paste thinly and cut out the leaf shape using either a maple leaf cutter or working with an exacto knife around a template (see page 85).

2 Rest the leaf on a foam pad and soften its edges using the ball tool.

3 Push 2 in. (5 cm) of 24 ga. wire up through the center of the leaf.

4 Emboss the leaf using a maple leaf veiner or a flower veining tool to imprint the leaf with veins.

5 Use the ball tool on the leaf edges to curl the leaf up.

6 Leave to dry, then use a paintbrush to dust the leaf with the various dusting powders to build up the fall shades.

Materials

- Gum paste
- Colorings
- Cornstarch (for dusting)
- 24 ga. wire
- Brown, classic gold and tangerine dusting powders
- Royal icing

Tools

- Workboard
- Rolling pin
- Maple leaf cutter
- Exacto knife
- Foam pad
- Ball tool
- Maple leaf veiner
- Paintbrush

Colors Used

3 oz. (90 g)

21 oak leaf

Combine with the maple leaf opposite to create a fall-themed cake.

Dust the center of the leaves with a darker dusting powder to add shadows.

1 Roll out 1 oz. (30 g) of green paste quite thinly and cut out two leaves using either an oak leaf cutter or cutting around a template (see page 85).

2 Insert 3 in. (7.5 cm) of 24 ga. green wire down the center of each leaf.

3 Soften the leaf on the foam pad using a bone tool and mark the veins using a flower veining

tool. Curl the leaf backward and leave to dry.

4 Shape ¼ oz. (10 g) of white paste into two cups. Insert a wire through the bottom of each cup and bend the wire over inside the cup to secure.

5 Make two acorn shapes, and secure them in the cups with edible glue.

6 Use a paintbrush to apply dusting powders to give realistic shades of color to the leaves and acorns.

Materials	Tools	Colors Used	
• Gum paste	• Workboard	● 2 oz. (60 g)	
• Colorings	• Rolling pin	○ ¼ oz. (7 g)	
• Cornstarch (for dusting)	• Oak leaf cutter		
• 24 ga. green wire	• Exacto knife		
• Edible glue	• Foam pad		
• Dark and leaf green dusting powders	• Bone tool		
	• Flower veining tool		
	• Paintbrush		

basic fruit

Place these pieces of fruit in the fruit bowl on page 131 to create the perfect topper for a fruit cake.

Tools

- Workboard
- Rolling pin
- Flower veining tool
- Pizza wheel
- Paintbrush
- Cone tool
- Ball tool
- Exacto knife
- Piping tube (No. 1)
- Piping bag

22

BANANA

1 Roll the white paste into a sausage shape. Make the ends of the sausage thinner than the center.

2 Texture the banana using the flower veining tool, running it down the length every ½ in. (1.5 cm). Curve the banana.

3 Roll out the yellow paste and use the pizza wheel to cut three ellipse shapes to make the three sections of skin. Place one under the banana, bending it back slightly as if the fruit has been peeled. Place the other two over the top, using edible glue to secure. Press together so there is no gap.

4 Squash the elements at the bottom of the banana together and paint with chestnut paste color in patches to finish.

Materials

Materials	Colors Used
• Gum paste	2 oz. (60 g)
• Colorings	2 oz. (60 g)
• Cornstarch (for dusting)	
• Edible glue	
• Chestnut paste color	

23

ORANGE

1 Shape the orange paste into a ball and press the sharp end of the cone tool into the center to indent.

2 Using the flower veining tool, indent the edges of the hole to make little creases toward the center.

3 Push a pinch of green paste into the hole then press gently with the ball tool to flatten.

4 Using the pointed end of the flower veining tool, prick the orange to give a "peel" effect.

5 Use the paintbrush to dust the surface of the orange with the tangerine dusting powder, making some areas darker than others.

Materials

Materials	Colors Used
• Gum paste	4 oz. (115 g)
• Colorings	Pinch
• Cornstarch (for dusting)	
• Tangerine dusting powder	

See also
Working with Color, pages 54–59 > Working with Gum Paste, pages 60–63 > Texturing, pages 74–81

APPLE

1 Roll 2½ oz. (75 g) of green paste into a ball, and use the ball tool to indent the apple top.

2 Roll out some of the remnants of paste and use an exacto knife to cut out a leaf shape. Texture the leaf with the flower veining tool.

3 Make an apple stalk with the remaining remnants of paste by rolling a tiny sausage around a strand of spaghetti. Push the stalk into the apple with the leaf at the side.

4 Use the paintbrush to dust the apple with green, chestnut and ruby dusting powders to finish.

STRAWBERRY

1 Model the strawberry from the red paste, pinching in around the lower section to achieve the classic strawberry shape.

2 Prick the paste all over with the end of the piping tube.

3 Roll out the green paste and use an exacto knife to cut out the stalk. Secure in place using edible glue.

4 Load the piping bag with sunflower royal icing and pipe tiny dots of icing into the pricked holes for seeds.

Materials	Colors used
• Gum paste	● 3 oz. (90 g)
• Colorings	
• Cornstarch (for dusting)	
• Dried spaghetti strand	
• Dusting powders	

Materials	Colors Used
• Gum paste	● 3 oz. (90 g)
• Colorings	● 1 oz. (30 g)
• Cornstarch (for dusting)	
• Edible glue	
• Sunflower royal icing	

26 grapes

A bunch of grapes sits well on a fruit cake.

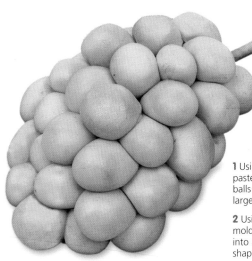

Dust the stalk to give it a more authentic look.

1 Using all of the green paste, make as many balls as you can, some large and some smaller.

2 Using edible glue, mold the balls together into a rough oval shape, then tweak and tease a little using the flower veining tool to give definition to each grape.

3 Shape the stalk from the cream paste and push it into the top of the bunch.

4 Use a paintbrush to dust the grapes with green dusting powder, making some darker than others, then dust areas of the cream stalk with chestnut to give depth.

Materials

- Gum paste
- Colorings
- Cornstarch (for dusting)
- Edible glue
- Green and chestnut dusting powders

Tools

- Workboard
- Flower veining tool
- Paintbrush

Colors Used

● 4 oz. (115 g)
○ 1 oz. (30 g)

27 blackberries

Blackberries are fiddly to make but are well worth the effort.

1 Make small cones of purple paste and secure onto short 24 ga. wires. Make tiny balls of purple paste and attach them to the cones using edible glue. As the balls build up, mold them together.

2 Roll out the green paste and use the calyx cutter to cut a calyx for each blackberry. Bend the calyx ends back using the bone tool on the foam pad. Attach with edible glue.

3 Use the rose leaf cutter to cut leaves, then insert wires into each leaf through the central vein. Press each leaf onto the leaf veiner.

4 Use a paintbrush to dust the leaves with green dusting powder.

5 Use stem tape to wire the berries and leaves together.

Materials	Tools	Colors Used
• Gum paste • Colorings • Cornstarch (for dusting) • 24 ga. green wire • Edible glue • Leaf green dusting powder • ¼ in. (5 mm) width stem tape	• Workboard • Paintbrush • Rolling pin • Calyx cutter • Bone tool • Foam pad • Rose leaf cutter • Leaf veiner	● 4 oz. (115 g) ● 3 oz. (90 g)

28 pineapple

This graphic pineapple would look great with the basic fruits on pages 126–127.

1 Shape the orange paste into an elongated oval. Flatten one end and sit the paste up on this end.

2 Using scissors, snip around the shape in a uniform pattern. Use the flower veining tool around the snips to make a squarish pattern.

3 Take pinches of leaf green paste and shape into teardrops, then use the flower veining tool to draw along each teardrop shape from the broad to the narrow end, and curl the narrow end out a little.

4 Insert short strands of spaghetti into the broad ends of the green leaves and insert these into the top of the pineapple.

5 Use a paintbrush and dusting powders to add deeper color to the leaves and fruit.

Materials

- Gum paste
- Colorings
- Cornstarch (for dusting)
- Spaghetti strands
- Tangerine, berberis and leaf green dusting powders

Tools

- Workboard
- Scissors
- Flower veining tool
- Paintbrush

Colors Used

- 2 oz. (60 g)
- 1 oz. (30 g)

29 fruit bowl

Show off your new fruit toppers in this neat fruit bowl.

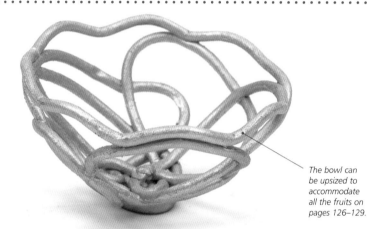

The bowl can be upsized to accommodate all the fruits on pages 126–129.

1 Soften the paste with shortening then extrude it through the extruder to form a long string of paste.

2 Dust the mold with cornstarch so the paste doesn't stick, and place it on a nonstick surface.

3 Coil the paste string over the sphere. Where the string crosses itself, secure with edible glue.

4 Bring all the ends to a finish at the top, and place a pad of paste over the ends. Make sure this is flat, because

it will form the base of the bowl.

5 Leave to dry, then carefully lift the paste off the mold and leave to dry a little longer.

6 Make a paint by mixing silver dusting

powder and vodka and apply to the fruit bowl using the paintbrush.

Materials	Tools	Colors Used
• Gum paste • Shortening • Cornstarch (for dusting) • Edible glue • Silver dusting powder • Vodka	• Workboard • Extruder with large single-hole disk • Mold, such as a tennis ball or small glass bowl • Paintbrush	3 oz. (90 g)

christmas leaves

Neat arrangements that a beginner can make for Christmas cakes.

Tools: Holly

- Workboard
- Rolling pin
- Holly leaf cutter (medium)
- Flower veining tool
- Paintbrush

UNWIRED HOLLY

1 Roll out the green paste on the workboard and use the holly leaf cutter to cut out approximately nine leaves.

2 Texture the leaves using the flower veining tool.

3 Roll the red paste into tiny berry shapes.

4 Secure the leaves and berries in an arrangement using edible glue. Bend and slightly twist the leaves to get a more realistic finish.

5 Paint the leaves and berries with edible glaze.

Materials	Colors Used
• Gum paste	🔴 2 oz. (60 g)
• Colorings	⚫ 1 oz. (30 g)
• Cornstarch (for dusting)	
• Edible glue	
• Edible glaze	

WIRED HOLLY

1 Roll out the green paste, but don't roll too thinly. Use the holly leaf cutter to cut out three leaves.

2 Texture the leaves using the flower veining tool.

3 Take a length of 24 ga. wire that is as long as the leaf and half as much again—about 3½ in. (9 cm)—and pierce the paste, pushing the wire up the length of the leaf, where the central stem runs. Curve the leaf back slightly and leave to dry.

4 Roll tiny berry shapes from the red paste.

5 Pierce the berries with small sections of 24 ga. wire.

6 Join all the pieces together using stem tape, stretching it slightly as you bind the items together.

7 Paint the leaves and berries with edible glaze.

Materials	Colors Used
• Flower paste or gum paste	🔴 2 oz. (60 g)
• Colorings	⚫ 1 oz. (30 g)
• Cornstarch (for dusting)	
• 24 ga. green wire	
• ¼ in. (5 mm) width stem tape	
• Edible glaze	

See also
Working with Color, pages 54–59 > Working with Gum Paste, pages 60–63 > Texturing, pages 74–81

Try making the flower from cream paste and painting with a gold paint.

Tools: Poinsettia

- Poinsettia cutters or template card, pencil and scissors
- Pizza wheel
- Exacto knife
- Foam pad
- Bone tool
- Poinsettia veiner or leaf veiner
- Paintbrush

Materials

- Flower paste or gum paste (with added gumtex)
- Coloring
- Cornstarch (for dusting)
- 24 ga. green wire
- Pollen powder or semolina
- ¼ in. (5 mm) width stem tape
- Green dusting powder (optional)

Colors Used

● 7 oz. (200 g)

WIRED POINSETTIA

1 Roll out the poinsettia paste thinly, making sure you dust with cornstarch first. Aim to cut out two or three bracts (poinsettia leaves) at a time, otherwise the paste will dry and crack before you have time to finish working on them.

2 If you are working from templates, use the pizza wheel to cut out the larger bracts and the exacto knife to cut out the smaller ones.

3 Place a bract onto the foam pad and soften the edges using the bone tool.

4 Thread a 24 ga. wire through the center of the bract. Vein using either the poinsettia veiner or a general leaf veiner. Leave to dry.

5 Make the remaining bracts, leaving the smallest until last, since these will be wired together while still soft so they conform to their neighboring bracts.

6 Using remnants of red paste, make small balls. Dip the balls into pollen powder or semolina to give them a burnished gold effect. Push them down the wires.

7 Wire the bracts together using stem tape, building up the poinsettia flower. Pull the stem tape slightly as you work, since this will make it stick to itself.

8 Use a paintbrush to dust a few of the leaves with green dusting powder if you wish.

33 santa

This Santa would make a cheerful addition to any Christmas cake.

Materials	Tools	Colors Used
• Gum paste • Colorings • Cornstarch (for dusting) • Edible glue • Dried spaghetti strands • Gold luster • Vodka	• Workboard • Flower veining tool • Paintbrush • Rolling pin • Exacto knife • Ball tool • Ribbon cutter	● 3 oz. (90 g) ● 1¼ oz. (37 g) ● 4½ oz. (130 g) ● 2 oz. (60 g) ● 1 oz. (30 g) ○ 4¾ oz. (135 g)

See also
Working with Color, pages 54–59 > Working with Gum Paste, pages 60–63 > Texturing, pages 74–81

MAKING THE BODY

4 Thinly roll out 1½ oz. (45 g) of red paste for the coat. Use the exacto knife to cut out a rectangle and wrap this around the body with the join at the front, overlapping slightly. Use the exacto knife to cut off excess paste. Pinch the paste at the shoulders and cut off any more excess paste.

5 Shape the arms from 1 oz. (30 g) of red paste. Roll into two sausages, then use the exacto knife to cut one end of each flat for the wrist and the opposite end at an angle for attachment at the shoulder. Fix the arm in place using edible glue. Use the flower veining tool to crease at the elbows. Allow one arm to rest on the leg, the other to dangle down beside the sack.

3 Shape the body from 2 oz. (60 g) of white paste. Push a spaghetti strand into the body ready to support the head.

2 Make two legs from 1 oz. (30 g) of red paste. Use edible glue to attach them to the top of the chimney (for how to make the chimney, see Step 14 on page 137), and use the flower veining tool to crease and fold the legs. Attach the boots to the bottom of the legs using edible glue. Push two spaghetti strands through the legs into the chimney for support of the body.

6 Use 1¼ oz. (37 g) of white paste to make fur trimmings for the coat and gloves. Shape them with the flower veining tool, using the flatter end to soften the appearance. Attach to the coat and cuffs using edible glue. Make the gloves using tiny balls of paste, and attach as before. Use a strand of spaghetti to assist positioning.

1 Shape two boots from 1 oz. (30 g) of black paste by forming a short sausage for each and bending them into a foot shape using the flower veining tool to assist.

Continued over the page ➡

9 Shape 1 oz. (30 g) of red paste into an elongated triangle for the hat. Stretch out the paste at the top and curl over using the flower veining tool. Use the ball tool to hollow out a space for the head. Attach white paste for trimming and a white ball of fur on the end of the hat. Attach to the head using edible glue. Support from behind until set.

ADDING DETAILS

8 Use edible glue to attach two tiny balls of leftover black paste to the face for eyes.

10 Make hair for the beard from 1 oz. (30 g) of white paste by rolling it out thinly and texturing using the flower veining tool. Use the exacto knife to trim the beard into a suitable shape. Attach the head to the body using dried spaghetti and edible glue, then attach the beard to the face. Make the mustache from small pinches of paste and texture as before.

7 Shape the head from 1 oz. (30 g) of flesh paste, pinching off a little for the nose (no need for ears—you don't see them). Attach the head over the spaghetti and with edible glue, then stick the nose on with more glue.

12 Make a paint by mixing gold luster dusting powder with vodka and use a paintbrush to apply this to the buckle.

11 Roll the remaining ¼ oz. (7 g) of black paste into a thin sausage, flatten it and roll smooth. Use the ribbon cutter to cut a thin ribbon for the black belt, and attach to the body using edible glue. Shape a buckle from a pinch of white paste, cut using the exacto knife and attach as before.

13 Shape a sack from the light brown paste and pinch at the top to form its neck. Indent the body of the sack with the flat end of the flower veining tool to give the impression of toys inside. Roll a thin sausage of leftover light brown paste and wrap it as a string around the top of the sack.

14 Form the chimney from 3 oz. (90 g) of terra cotta paste, shaping it into an elongated cube. Use the flower veining tool to imprint the chimney with a brick pattern. Leave to dry.

34 christmas tree

A delicate-looking tree but, with a little care, so easy to make.

Materials	Tools	Colors Used
• Gum paste • Fondant • Colorings • Cornstarch (for dusting) • Holly green royal icing • Snowflake luster	• Workboard • Rolling pin • Spacers • Template card, pencil and scissors • Pizza wheel • Exacto knife • Emery board • Piping tube (No. 1.5) • Piping bag • Small snowflake cutter • Paintbrush	Gum paste: ● 5 oz. (140 g) ○ 2 oz. (60 g) Fondant: ○ 1 oz. (30 g)

See also
Working with Color, pages 54–59 > Working with Gum Paste, pages 60–63 > Templates, pages 250–251

2 Once dry, sand the edges gently using the emery board.

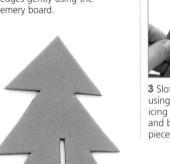

3 Slot the full pieces together using small dots of green royal icing applied with a piping tube and bag. Attach the half tree pieces in the same way.

1 Roll out the green paste between spacers to achieve the same depth for each element of the tree. Using the Christmas tree template (see page 251), pizza wheel and exacto knife, cut out one shape of each full tree, one with a slit at the top and one with a slit at the bottom. Cut out four half shapes. Leave them all to dry on a flat surface.

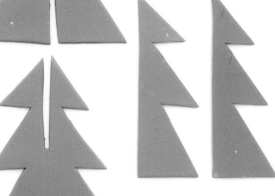

4 Place the tree on a pad of white fondant, pressing it gently into the paste to give more support. Leave to dry thoroughly.

8 Use a paintbrush to dust the white decorations with snowflake luster, and sprinkle over the tree to complete.

7 Cut out snowflakes using the snowflake cutter and attach to the tree as before.

6 Make baubles and attach using royal icing.

5 Roll out a thin sausage of white paste. Flatten the sausage at intervals with the rolling pin to create a decorative string to attach to the tree with royal icing. String it along the branches of the tree.

35 angel

The charming trio of angels are singing their hearts out for Christmas.
The ingredients listed here will make just one of the characters.

Materials

- Gum paste
- Flower paste
- Colorings
- Cornstarch (for dusting)
- Dried spaghetti strands
- Edible glue
- Shortening
- 26 ga. silver wire
- Royal icing

Tools

- Workboard
- Rolling pin
- Large blossom cutter
- Foam pad
- Bone tool
- Exacto knife
- Flower veining tool
- Semicircle tool
- Paintbrush
- Extruder with multihole disk
- Toothpick

Colors Used

Gum paste:
- 4¼ oz. (122 g)
- 1 oz. (30 g)
- ¼ oz. (7 g)

Flower paste:
- 1 oz. (30 g)

See also
Working with Color, pages 54–59 > Working with Gum Paste, pages 60–63 > Texturing, pages 74–81

5 Shape ¾ oz. (20 g) of flesh-colored paste into an egg shape for the head. Mark the mouth with the flower veining tool and fix three balls of flesh-colored paste as ears and a nose. Use the semicircle tool to mark closed eyes. Use edible glue to fix the head over a spaghetti strand. Leave to dry.

4 Shape the hands from ¼ oz. (7 g) of flesh-colored paste by rolling them into teardrops, flattening the broad ends and cutting fingers using the exacto knife. Attach the hands to the cuffs.

3 Shape the arms from 1 oz. (30 g) of white paste. Shape the paste into two triangles. Elongate one point to create the shoulder, flatten the shape and attach to the side of the body, allowing the cuff section to protrude. Push spaghetti strands into the cuffs in preparation for the hands.

2 Thinly roll out 1 oz. (30 g) of white paste then cut out a large blossom shape. Place on a foam pad and soften the edges with the bone tool.

1 Shape 1½ oz. (45 g) of white paste into a cone with a flattened top.

6 Make the hair from ¾ oz. (20 g) of paste in a color of your choosing. Mix the paste with a little shortening to soften it, then extrude it through the multihole disk in the extruder and secure with edible glue.

7 Bend the silver wire in half and twist together. Wrap around a rolling pin to create a halo. Twist the ends together and push them into the back of the head.

8 Thinly roll out 1 oz. (30 g) of flower paste and cut out wing shapes using the exacto knife. Place each wing in turn on the foam pad and frill using the toothpick. Attach in place with dots of royal icing.

9 Cut out a book shape from the yellow paste and attach to the hands with more glue.

36 snowman

The perfect topper for the perfect Christmas cake. Add snowballs made of royal icing to the base of the cake to set the scene.

Materials	Tools	Colors Used
• Gum paste	• Workboard	○ 4 oz. (115 g)
• Colorings	• Exacto knife	◐ ¼ oz. (7 g)
• Cornstarch (for dusting)	• Piping tube (small)	● ½ oz. (15 g)
• Dried spaghetti strands	• Flower veining tool	● 1 oz. (30 g)
• Edible glue	• Rolling pin	● ¼ oz. (7 g)
• Confectioners' sugar (for decoration)	• Paintbrush	● ¼ oz. (7 g)
		○ 1¼ oz. (37 g)

See also
Working with Color, pages 54–59 > Working with Gum Paste, pages 60–63 > Texturing, pages 74–81

EASY

4 Make the nose from the orange paste, molded into a carrot shape and indented with the flower veining tool. Attach to the face using a strand of dried spaghetti. Using a pinch of black, shape the eyes.

5 Make three berries from the red paste. Roll the green paste thinly, then use the large end of the piping tube to cut curves off the paste to make tiny holly leaves. Imprint veins on the leaf using the flower veining tool.

3 Shape 1 oz. (30 g) of white paste into the head, attach it to the body over the spaghetti strands, then use the large end of the piping tube to imprint a smiling mouth.

6 Shape the orange-brown paste into the hat by making a large brim to fit over the snowman's head. Then make the rest of the hat separately. Pinch in the edges of the pointed hat section a little to give it an old look, and attach to the brim with edible glue.

2 Make two arms from 1 oz. (30 g) of white paste. Roll it out into a sausage shape, then cut in half using the exacto knife. Flatten one end of each arm and attach this end to the shoulders of the snowman.

1 Make the snowman's body from 2 oz. (60 g) of white paste. Make an oval and flatten out one end. Stand the body upright and push dried spaghetti strands into the neck ready to support the head.

8 Shape three buttons from the black paste. Attach down the front of the snowman using edible glue.

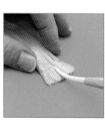

7 Combine green, red and yellow paste to give a multicolored paste. Roll it into a long sausage and cut off a section to wrap around the snowman's neck. Cut the remaining length into two and frill one end of each using the exacto knife. Tuck one under the scarf and place one over the scarf, at the join, and fix with edible glue.

37 skating penguins

Such cute little creatures, these would make fantastic toppers for a Christmas cake, or even for a themed birthday cake.

Materials

- Gum paste
- Cornstarch (for dusting)
- Edible glue
- Dried spaghetti strands
- Silver dusting powder
- Vodka

Tools

- Workboard
- Rolling pin
- Exacto knife
- Paintbrush
- Flower veining tool

Colors Used

- 2 oz. (60 g)
- 2 oz. (60 g)
- ½ oz. (15 g)

See also
Working with Color, pages 54–59 > Working with Gum Paste, pages 60–63 > Texturing, pages 74–81

2 Thinly roll out ¾ oz. (20 g) of black paste and shape it into a large teardrop. Wrap this shape around the penguin body to check for size. Trim with the exacto knife if necessary. When you are happy with the shape, attach it to the back of the penguin using edible glue, allowing the pointed end to drape over the center of the face, to give the distinctive penguin look.

3 Use remnants of black paste to make two black eyes and attach with more glue.

4 Shape the beak from ⅜ oz. (6 g) of orange paste. Start with a triangle, soften the edges, then use the exacto knife to cut through to shape the top and bottom of the beak. Sharpen the beak by pinching the top and bottom to points. Attach to the face using edible glue.

1 Put a pinch of white paste aside for the skates. Shape the remaining white paste into an egg shape. Bend the shape at the center. Curve the narrow end—this will form the head.

5 Make wings from ¼ oz. (7 g) of black paste. Shape into egg shapes and flatten. Attach using edible glue.

7 Make skates from the white paste saved in Step 1. Shape four small balls, then roll the remaining paste quite thickly and cut two short blades. Attach the balls to the feet first using edible glue, then attach the blades to the balls. Mix silver dusting powder with vodka and use a paintbrush to apply the resulting silver paint to the blades.

6 Trim the orange paste into thick rectangles for the feet. Narrow one end of the shape and soften the edges. Indent the toes using the flower veining tool. Push two short spaghetti strands into the bottom of the penguin's body. Make two legs from small balls of orange paste, then thread the legs and feet onto the spaghetti.

38 diwali diva lamp

The perfect topper for the perfect cake to celebrate Diwali.

Materials

- Gum paste
- Coloring
- Cornstarch (for dusting)
- Edible glue
- Shortening
- Red, orange, yellow and gold dusting powders
- Piping gel
- Vodka

Tools

- Workboard
- Rolling pin
- 4 in. (10 cm) round cutter
- Pizza wheel
- 1 pint (500 ml) glass bowl
- Small pearl mold
- Extruder with tiny single-hole disk
- Paper towel
- Paintbrush

Colors Used

- 3½ oz. (105 g)

See also
Working with Color, pages 54–59 > Working with Gum Paste, pages 60–63 > Texturing, pages 74–81

5 Shape ½ oz. (15 g) of paste into a conical shape for the flame, and leave to dry.

3 Replace the cutter on the paste circle to see where the distortion is, slightly indent the cutter and, using the pizza wheel, cut a point in the circle.

4 Turn a small glass bowl upside down and dust with cornstarch. Place the paste circle over the bowl and mold it to the shape of the base. Leave to dry.

6 Make a string of pearls using the pearl mold, and attach to the edge of the lamp with edible glue.

2 Place the rolling pin back onto the paste circle and roll a small section to change the shape from an even circle to a slightly elongated one.

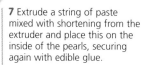

7 Extrude a string of paste mixed with shortening from the extruder and place this on the inside of the pearls, securing again with edible glue.

1 Roll out 2½ oz. (75 g) of paste and use the 4 in. (10 cm) round cutter to cut out one circle.

8 Place the conical shape on the pointed edge of the burner, secure with edible glue and support with a paper towel until dry. Use a paintbrush and dusting powders to color the conical "flame" using red in the center, getting lighter toward the edge.

9 To finish the topper off, add small amounts of classic gold dusting powder to piping gel until a shining gel is achieved. Tip this into the burner with a small track of "oil" leading up to the flame. Finish the burner off by painting the pearls with a paint made from gold dusting powder and vodka.

39 easter bunny

A cute little white bunny enjoying a snack. This topper uses bought chocolate eggs, but you could make your own, or make a little hill out of fondant.

Materials

- Gum paste
- Colorings
- Cornstarch (for dusting)
- Edible glue
- Dried spaghetti strands

Tools

- Workboard
- Flower veining tool
- Paintbrush
- Exacto knife

Colors Used

- 6½ oz. (185 g)
- 1 oz. (30 g)
- ½ oz. (15 g)
- ¼ oz. (7 g)
- ¼ oz. (7 g)
- Pinch

See also
Working with Color, pages 54–59 > Working with Gum Paste, pages 60–63 > Texturing, pages 74–81

EASY

5 For each ear, shape ½ oz. (15 g) of white paste into a teardrop. Copy the shape with the remaining pink paste to make the ear inserts, and attach with edible glue. Fix the ears to the head using edible glue, and support until dry.

6 Make hair strands from pinches of white paste, and use the flower veining tool to texture the hair. Attach to the head using edible glue.

7 Make a bow using the purple paste, and attach with edible glue.

8 Make eyes and eyebrows using a pinch of black paste, and attach with edible glue. Make the nose from a pinch of pink paste, and secure with edible glue. Make two cheeks from ¼ oz. (7 g) of white paste, attach to the face using edible glue, then texture by pricking with the pointed end of the flower veining tool.

4 Shape a teardrop for the head from 1 oz. (30 g) of white paste. Push it onto the spaghetti strands and secure with edible glue.

3 Make the body from 2½ oz. (75 g) of white paste. Shape it into a basic triangle and bend the shape slightly at the waist. Push strands of dried spaghetti through the neck ready for the head.

9 Use ½ oz. (15 g) of white paste for each of the arms, rolling them into a rough sausage and attaching to the body using edible glue.

2 Make pink pads from ¼ oz. (7 g) of pink paste: three tiny balls and one larger ball for each pad. Flatten the balls onto the feet, securing with edible glue.

10 Make the carrot from orange paste. Texture it with the exacto knife. Shape green paste into small teardrops, and texture with the flower veining tool to create leaves. Attach with edible glue.

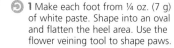

1 Make each foot from ¼ oz. (7 g) of white paste. Shape into an oval and flatten the heel area. Use the flower veining tool to shape paws.

40 valentine hearts

A quick, simple and romantic cake topper.

Materials	Tools
• Flower paste or gum paste (with added gumtex)	• Workboard
	• Rolling pin
• Colorings	• Various heart-shaped cutters (large and small)
• Cornstarch (for dusting)	
• Edible glue	• Paper and pencil (optional)
• Royal icing (optional)	• Flower veining tool
	• Paper towel

Colors Used

○ 3 oz. (90 g)
● 1 oz. (30 g)

See also
Working with Color, pages 54–59 > Working with Gum Paste, pages 60–63 > Templates, pages 250–251

3 Cut five large and small hearts from the deep red paste. Allow the hearts to dry thoroughly before attempting to finish this decoration. The stability of the topper relies on the hearts being dry.

4 Either follow the pattern shown on the cake opposite, or work out your own on paper before placing on the cake.

2 Cut out eight large and small hearts from the dusky pink paste. For the largest hearts, cut further smaller hearts out of their centers to allow other hearts to be seen behind them.

5 Work from the back to the front of the topper, starting with the largest heart first.

6 Position the hearts on soft paste—indent the paste to mark the position, and deepen the indentation with the flower veining tool.

1 Roll out both paste colors quite thinly using the rolling pin.

7 Apply a little edible glue to the slot and then insert the heart. Support it from behind with a rolled up piece of paper towel until firm.

fireworks

Collectively, these make a fantastic topper for a Canada Day or an Independence Day celebration.

Tools

- Workboard
- Paintbrush
- Rolling pin
- Star cutter
- Exacto knife
- Ruler
- Flower veining tool

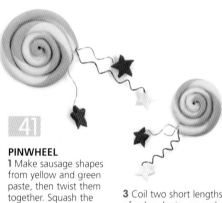

41

PINWHEEL

1 Make sausage shapes from yellow and green paste, then twist them together. Squash the shape and roll it up into a pinwheel, securing as you roll with dots of edible glue.

2 Roll out the red and white pastes and use the star cutter to cut out a red and a white star.

3 Coil two short lengths of colored wire around the paintbrush to form a "spring" shape. Insert the wires into the end of the pinwheel, and attach the stars to the ends of the wires using edible glue.

42

ROMAN CANDLE

1 Twist the two colors of paste together, trying not to work them too much and lose the swirled design.

2 Roll the paste into a sausage shape and use an exacto knife to cut to length.

3 Push a small length of 24 ga. wire into one end for the fuse.

When coloring the paste, don't work the colors all the way into the paste; instead aim for swirls of color.

Materials

- Gum paste
- Colorings
- Cornstarch (for dusting)
- 24 ga. colored wire
- Edible glue

Colors Used

- ⬤ Pinch
- ⬤ Pinch
- ⬤ Pinch
- ⬤ Pinch

Materials

- ¼ oz. (10 g) gum paste
- Colorings
- Cornstarch (for dusting)
- 24 ga. wire

Colors Used

- ⬤ Pinch
- ⬤ Pinch

See also
Working with Color, pages 54–59 > Working with Gum Paste, pages 60–63 > Texturing, pages 74–81

43

ROCKET

1 Roll out the white paste. Use the star cutter to cut two stars. Shape the remaining white paste into the body of the rocket.

2 Shape a pinch of the red paste, but not all of it, into the rocket cone.

3 Push a spaghetti strand into the top of the rocket body, add a little edible glue then push the rocket cone onto the body.

4 Roll out a pinch of red, orange and yellow paste. Use the exacto knife to cut out rocket flames, making each

one smaller than the last. Secure together using edible glue.

5 Shape the remaining red paste into a ribbon to wrap around the body of the rocket.

6 To attach the flames to the bottom of rocket, use the exacto knife to slit the base of the rocket body and slide the flames inside.

7 Coil lengths of wire around the paintbrush to form a "spring" shape. Push the coiled wires into the base of the rocket. Attach the stars with edible glue.

44

FIREWORKS BOX

1 Shape 3 oz. (90 g) of dark gold paste into a box shape.

2 Roll out 1 oz. (30 g) of dark gold paste and use the exacto knife to cut two box ends.

3 Texture the two sections to look like wood, using a ruler and the flower veining tool. Attach to the ends of the box shape using edible glue.

4 Roll out the remaining dark gold paste to make the front and back of the box. Texture as before. Fix to the box with edible glue.

5 Using the light gold paste, cut one plank of wood for the front of the box. Attach with edible glue.

6 When the plank is dry, use a paintbrush and red paste color to paint words onto it.

7 Cut offcuts of paste into thin strips of various lengths and widths to make packing material for the box.

Materials	Colors Used
• Gum paste	¼ oz. (7 g)
• Colorings	Pinch
• Cornstarch	Pinch
• 24 ga. wire	Pinch
• Dried spaghetti strand	
• Edible glue	

Materials	Colors Used
• Gum paste	6 oz. (170 g)
• Colorings	1 oz. (30 g)
• Cornstarch (for dusting)	
• Edible glue	
• Red paste color	

pumpkins

A rather mixed bunch of characters here! Choose your favorite and either smile or scream!

45

PEAR-SHAPED PUMPKIN

1 Shape the orange paste into a ball, then elongate the top section to give the pumpkin a longer appearance.

2 Use the flower veining tool to texture the segments of the pumpkin, then push in the top of the pumpkin.

3 Use the veining tool to make sockets for the eyes.

4 Shape the outline of the mouth and nose with the exacto knife, then use the veining tool to indent the paste.

5 Insert black paste into the mouth and eyes and attach a black nose using edible glue.

6 Shape the stalk from some of the green paste. Use offcuts to make two oval leaf shapes. Texture the veins using the flower veining tool and secure with edible glue.

46

SCARY PUMPKIN

1 Shape the orange paste into a ball.

2 Use the flower veining tool to texture the segments.

3 Push in the top of the pumpkin to give a flattened appearance.

4 Use the veining tool to make eye sockets.

5 Shape the outline of the mouth and nose with the exacto knife, and use the veining tool to indent the paste.

6 Insert black paste into the mouth, eyes and nose.

7 Cut two triangular eyebrows and secure with edible glue.

8 Make the pumpkin stalk from black paste, using the flower veining tool to texture the sides. Use offcuts to make tendrils by making "worms" of paste; smooth in the palm of your hand to coil. Stick in place using edible glue.

Materials	Colors Used
• Gum paste	● 1 oz. (30 g)
• Colorings	○ 1 oz. (30 g)
• Cornstarch (for dusting)	● 4 oz. (115 g)
• Edible glue	

Materials	Colors Used
• Gum paste	● 2 oz. (60 g)
• Colorings	○ 4 oz. (115 g)
• Cornstarch (for dusting)	
• Edible glue	

See also
Working with Color, pages 54–59 > Working with Gum Paste, pages 60–63 > Texturing, pages 74–81

WITCH'S HAT PUMPKIN

1 Shape the orange paste into a ball.

2 Use the flower veining tool to texture the segments, then push in the top of the pumpkin to give a flattened appearance.

3 Use the veining tool to make sockets for the eyes.

4 Shape the outline of the mouth and nose with the exacto knife, then use the veining tool to indent the paste.

5 Insert black paste into the mouth, eyes and nose.

6 Make the hat by shaping the purple paste in a cone shape. Smooth out and thin the base to make the frilled edge of the brim. Lengthen out the top and twist into a jaunty position.

7 Use the remaining black paste to make a band around the hat and cut to trim. Use the yellow paste to shape the buckle.

TOOTHY PUMPKIN

1 Shape the orange paste into a ball and pinch off a tiny amount for the nose.

2 Use the flower veining tool to texture the segments, then push in the top of the pumpkin to give a flattened look.

3 Use the veining tool to texture the wiggly mouth and make large triangular sockets for the eyes.

4 Shape the nose into a cone and bend using the veining tool. Attach with edible glue.

5 Push balls of white paste into the eye sockets, then shape a tooth and attach with edible glue.

6 Push a small ball of black paste into the corner of each eye for the pupils.

7 Make the pumpkin stalk using the green paste and the flower veining tool to texture the sides. Use offcuts to make tendrils by modeling "worms" of paste and smoothing them in the palm of your hand to form coils. Fix with edible glue.

Materials	Colors Used
• Gum paste	● ¾ oz. (20 g)
• Colorings	● 4 oz. (115 g)
• Cornstarch (for	● ¼ oz. (7 g)
dusting)	● 1 oz. (30 g)
• Edible glue	

Materials	Colors Used
• Gum paste	○ ½ oz. (15 g)
• Colorings	● ¼ oz. (7 g)
• Cornstarch (for	● 1¼ oz. (37 g)
dusting)	● 4 oz. (115 g)
• Edible glue	

49 witch

A spooky witch topper suitable for a halloween-themed cake.

Materials	Tools	Colors Used
• Gum paste	• Workboard	⬤ 8½ oz (240 g)
• Colorings	• Paintbrush	⬤ ¾ oz. (20 g)
• Cornstarch (for dusting)	• Flower veining tool	⚪ ¼ oz. (7 g)
• Dried spaghetti strands	• Exacto knife	⚪ 2 oz. (60 g)
• Edible glue	• Piping tube	
	• Rolling pin	

See also
Working with Color, pages 54–59 > Working with Gum Paste, pages 60–63 > Texturing, pages 74–81

2 Shape the arms from ¾ oz. (20 g) of black paste. Attach using edible glue to the shoulders. Push a spaghetti strand into the end of each arm. Support the arm in an upright position until dry. Shape two hands from the flesh paste. Use the flower veining tool and the exacto knife to form thumbs and fingers. Attach the hands to the arms, pushing them onto the spaghetti strands and securing with edible glue.

3 Shape 1 oz. (30 g) of black paste into a witch's hat. Cut a strip of red paste long enough to form a band for the hat. Wrap the band around the hat and secure with edible glue. Make a buckle for the band from black paste and fix in place with more glue.

4 Shape the head, nose and ears from 1½ oz. (45 g) of flesh paste, and attach the nose and ears using edible glue. Mark the mouth with the broad end of the piping tube.

5 Add two tiny warts to the face. Attach the head to the body and the hat to the head.

1 Shape the body from 2 oz. (60 g) of black paste, divided into two. Form a rough conical shape but with a flattened top. Shape the chest section to give a bust line. Push three spaghetti strands through the shape leaving ⅜ in. (1 cm) protruding to support the head.

6 Roll out ½ oz. (15 g) of black paste, then texture with the flower veining tool to give pleats to the skirt. Use the exacto knife to trim the skirt into a rectangle, then scrunch together. Neaten the top of the skirt with a thin strip of black paste.

9 Roll out 3 oz. (90 g) of black paste. Use the exacto knife to cut a rectangle for the cape. Paint edible glue over the back of the witch. Wrap the cape around the body, pinching it in around the neck. Make a thin string of black paste to form a bow.

7 Pinch off six balls of red and six of white paste. Take two strands of spaghetti. Pierce the balls, one red then one white, to give striped stockings, putting a dab of edible glue between each ball. When stacked up, roll slightly to flatten and squash the balls together. Leave ⅜ in. (1 cm) of spaghetti sticking out. Secure to the front of the witch's body with edible glue and fix the skirt on top.

8 Shape two shoes and two buckles from ¾ oz. (20 g) of black paste.

50 ghost

This phantom is a reminder of childhood Halloweens, when dressing up as a ghost meant putting a sheet over your head.

Materials

- Gum paste
- Colorings
- Cornstarch (for dusting)
- Dried spaghetti strands

Tools

- Workboard
- Rolling pin
- Ball tool
- Flower veining tool
- Exacto knife

Colors Used

- 7 oz. (200 g)
- Pinch

See also
Working with Color, pages 54–59 > Working with Gum Paste, pages 60–63 > Texturing, pages 74–81

3 Use the ball tool to shape the mouth into a open oval. Use the pointed end of the flower veining tool to shape the teardrop eyes. Fill the eyes and mouth with a pinch of black paste.

4 Use the remaining white paste for the two hands. Shape the paste into an oval, then use the exacto knife to cut the fingers—here only three—and thumb. Attach the hands to the body using dried spaghetti strands to support, then, using the flatter end of the flower veining tool, rub the paste at the base of the hands to blend with the body.

1 Make the basic shape from 4 oz. (115 g) of white paste molded into a "torpedo" shape. Flatten the bottom and stand upright. Leave to dry.

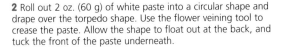

2 Roll out 2 oz. (60 g) of white paste into a circular shape and drape over the torpedo shape. Use the flower veining tool to crease the paste. Allow the shape to float out at the back, and tuck the front of the paste underneath.

potions and spells

Here are a few ideas to add to a Halloween cake.

POTION BOTTLE

1 Take the green paste, pinch a small amount off, then model the remainder into a bottle shape, starting with a teardrop.

2 Roll the pinch of green paste into a tiny sausage, flatten slightly and trim the sides with the exacto knife. Attach with edible glue around the top of bottle to make a rim.

3 Shape the yellow paste into a stopper and attach to the bottle rim using edible glue.

BUBBLING BOTTLE

1 Shape 1 oz. (30 g) of red paste into a rectangle and pinch the sides to make it sharper. Stand upright.

2 Using ¼ oz. (7 g) of red paste, shape the neck of the bottle and fix in place with edible glue.

3 Shape the stopper using ¾ oz. (20 g) of red paste, pinching the edges as before.

4 Make bubbles using the white paste. Shape the paste into balls and stick in place using edible glue, then use the flower veining tool to squish them together.

Materials	Colors Used
• Gum paste	● 1 oz. (30 g)
• Colorings	◐ ¼ oz. (7 g)
• Cornstarch (for dusting)	
• Edible glue	

Materials	Colors Used
• Gum paste	● 2 oz. (60 g)
• Colorings	○ ½ oz. (15 g)
• Cornstarch (for dusting)	
• Edible glue	

See also
Working with Color, pages 54–59 > Working with Gum Paste, pages 60–63 > Texturing, pages 74–81

53

54

CAULDRON

1 Shape 1½ oz. (45 g) of black paste into a ball. Flatten the top and bottom.

2 Roll ¼ oz. (7 g) of black paste into a sausage and place on top of the cauldron lip. Trim to fit.

3 Roll ¼ oz. (7 g) of black paste into another sausage for the cauldron handle. Wrap around the side of the cauldron and secure with edible glue.

4 Add "rivets" to the cauldron handle using two balls of black paste.

5 Fill the cauldron with piping gel.

STACK OF BOOKS

1 Shape the paste for the pages into a rectangle: large book 1¼ x 1½ in. (3 x 4 cm); medium book 1½ x ¾ in. (4 x 2 cm); green book 1 x ½ in. (2 x 1 cm); purple book ½ x ½ in. (1.5 x 1.5 cm). Score the sides using the exacto knife to create "pages."

2 Roll out the binding paste in a rectangle that is slightly larger than the pages. Wrap around the pages and attach with edible glue.

Materials	Colors Used
• Gum paste	● 2 oz. (60 g)
• Colorings	
• Cornstarch (for dusting)	
• Edible glue	
• Piping gel	

Materials	Colors Used
• Gum paste	○ 4½ oz. (130 g)
• Colorings	▨ 1 oz. (30 g)
• Cornstarch (for dusting)	● 1 oz. (30 g)
• Edible glue	● ½ oz. (15 g)
	● ½ oz. (15 g)

55 bride and groom 1

The traditional wedding cake topper features the bride and groom dressed as the happy couple are on the day. It makes a wonderful keepsake.

Materials

- Gum paste
- Flower paste
- Colorings
- Cornstarch (for dusting)
- Edible glue
- Dried spaghetti strands
- Shortening

Tools

- Workboard
- Piping tube
- Paintbrush
- Ball tool
- Extruder with multihole disk
- Rolling pin
- Exacto knife
- 1 mm pearl mold
- Flower veining tool
- Pizza wheel
- Toothpick
- Textured rolling pin
- Foam pad

Colors Used

For the bride:

Gum paste:

- 1½ oz. (45 g)
- 1 oz. (30 g)
- 1 oz. (30 g)
- Pinch
- ¾ oz. (20 g)

Flower paste:

- 1½ oz. (45 g)

For the groom:

Gum paste:

- 1¾ oz. (50 g)
- 2 oz. (60 g)
- 1 oz. (30 g)
- 1 oz. (30 g)
- 1 oz. (30 g)
- ½ oz. (15 g)

Flower paste:

- 1 oz. (30 g)

See also

Designing Your Cake, pages 26–31 > Working with Color, pages 54–59 > Working with Gum Paste, pages 60–63 > Making Basic Figures, pages 68–73

MAKING THE BRIDE'S BODY

3 For the head, form ½ oz. (15 g) of flesh-colored paste into a rough almond shape, the narrower end being the chin. Mark the mouth and eyes using the piping tube. Insert a spaghetti strand into the bride's body to support the head, then fix the head in place over the spaghetti, and secure with edible glue.

2 Make the bust section from ¾ oz. (20 g) of flesh paste, shaping the neck down to the waist, and taking care not to overdo the bust area. Attach to the base over the spaghetti strand using edible glue. Leave to dry.

1 Shape the flower paste into the base of the figure by forming a cone and flattening the top. Insert a spaghetti strand into the top of the cone.

4 Make the eyes from a pinch of black paste and attach with edible glue.

5 Make two ears from a pinch of flesh-colored paste rolled into two balls. Indent the ears using the small end of the ball tool and attach to the head with more glue. Add a pinch of flesh-colored paste to the center of the face to form the nose.

6 Make the arms from ¼ oz. (7 g) of flesh-colored paste. Roll thin, delicate arms, and flatten one end for hands. Attach the arms to the body using edible glue.

7 Make the bride's hair by extruding the brown paste mixed with shortening through the extruder to give strands of paste. Secure these to the head using edible glue.

Continued over the page →

CLOTHING THE BRIDE

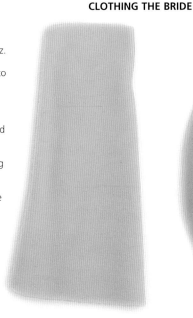

8 Thinly roll out 1 oz. (30 g) of pale pink paste. Use the exacto knife to cut a neat edge for the top of the dress. Fit the dress to the body, placing the neatened edge to the top of the bride, then secure in place using edible glue. Use the exacto knife to cut off the excess at the back, creating a seam. Neaten the bottom of the dress section using the exacto knife blade.

10 Use any leftover paste to make the "pearl" trims. Place a thin sausage of paste into the pearl mold and press firmly together. Remove the string of pearls from the mold, trim off the excess with the exacto knife and attach using edible glue.

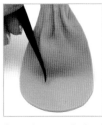

9 For the train, thinly roll out 1 oz. (30 g) of dark pink paste and shape into a rectangle. Mold one short end into a curved shape. Attach the other end to the back of the figure, at hip level, gathering paste as you go. Use the flower veining tool to tweak the paste so it folds. Secure in place with edible glue.

11 Make the bouquet of flowers by rolling out pale pink remnants thinly. Use the pizza wheel to cut strips, then roll up each strip, pleating the paste as you work. Pinch the base of the paste together to keep the shape. Make several flowers of different sizes by rolling more or less paste to make large or small flowers. Use edible glue to fix the flowers around the hands and on the dress.

12 Make further flowers to cascade around the edges and back of the dress, neatening the join of the train to the dress. Secure as before.

13 A textured section could be added to the bodice using dark pink remnants to match the pattern of the real bride's dress.

14 Make four tiny pale pink buttons and fix to the back of the top of the dress with edible glue.

15 To finish the dress, cut a short strip of dark pink paste. Frill one edge on the foam pad using the toothpick and attach under the flowers using edible glue.

Continued over the page ➡

MAKING THE GROOM'S BODY

19 Using a pinch of black paste, make two tiny eyes and secure to the face using edible glue.

18 For the head, form ½ oz. (15 g) of flesh-colored paste into a rough almond shape, the narrower end being the chin. Mark the mouth and eyes using the piping tube. Fix the head in place over the spaghetti strand on the body and secure with edible glue.

20 Make the groom's hair by extruding the black paste mixed with shortening through the extruder to give strands of paste. Secure these to the head using edible glue.

21 Make two ears from ⅛ oz. (3.5 g) of flesh paste. Indent each ear with the smaller end of the ball tool and attach to the side of the head using edible glue.

22 Before making the arms and hands, you will need to clothe the groom (see Steps 25–29 opposite). Roll ¼ oz. (7 g) of the gray paste (see Step 28) into a thin sausage and use the exacto knife to cut it in half for the arms. Flatten one end of each arm and attach this end to the shoulders using edible glue. Push a spaghetti strand into each wrist.

17 For the body, shape 1 oz. (30 g) of white paste into an oval. Flatten one end and push this end onto the spaghetti on top of the legs, using edible glue to secure. Push a strand of spaghetti into the neck section and leave standing to dry.

23 Shape the hands from ¼ oz. (7 g) of flesh paste, and attach to the wrists over the spaghetti strands, using edible glue to secure.

16 Roll the black flower paste into a long sausage shape for the legs. Use the exacto knife to cut the sausage into two equal lengths, then glue them together with edible glue. Push a strand of spaghetti into each end of each leg and lay flat to dry.

24 Use ¼ oz. (7 g) of black paste for the shoes. Shape two teardrops and push them onto the spaghetti strands in the legs. Fix with edible glue. Stand up and support upright until dry.

CLOTHING THE GROOM

25 For the shirt collar, roll out ¼ oz. (7 g) of white paste, then use the exacto knife to cut a thin strip, ⅛ in. (2.5 mm) wide. Angle the ends to make the wing collar. Attach to the neck using edible glue with the collar wings at the front.

29 Use remnants of pale pink paste to make a cravat. Shape the paste into a rough diamond and texture it with the flower veining tool. Attach to the front of the figure using edible glue. Add a ball of paste for the cravat's knot.

26 Thinly roll out the dark pink paste and use the exacto knife to cut out the waistcoat shapes. Texture with a textured rolling pin if you wish. Attach the waistcoat to the front of the figure using edible glue, overlapping the edges slightly.

27 Make four tiny pale pink buttons and fix to the front of the waistcoat with more glue.

28 Blend ¾ oz. (20 g) of white paste with the remaining black paste for the coat and arms. Roll out 1 oz. (30 g) of this gray paste into a rectangular shape and attach around the body, using edible glue to secure. Curl back the front for coat lapels.

56 bride and groom 2

If you are making a cuddling couple, prepare each figure, but omit the arms on both. Fix the bride's arms first then position and complete the groom.

Materials	Tools
• Gum paste	• Workboard
• Flower paste	• Paintbrushes
• Colorings	• Piping tube
• Cornstarch (for dusting)	• Ball tool
• Dried spaghetti strands	• Extruder with multihole disk
• Edible glue	• Rolling pin
• Shortening	• Fabric-effect embossing tool
• Gold luster	• Ribbon cutter
• Vodka	• Flower veining tool
	• Pizza wheel

Colors Used

For the bride:	For the groom:
Gum paste:	Gum paste:
● 2 oz. (60 g)	● 1½ oz. (45 g)
● 4 oz. (115 g)	○ 1 oz. (30 g)
● 1 oz. (30 g)	● 1 oz. (30 g)
	● 2¾ oz. (82 g)
Flower paste:	● ¼ oz. (7 g)
○ 1½ oz. (45 g)	
	Flower paste:
	○ ½ oz. (15 g)

See also
Designing Your Cake, pages 26–31 > Working with Color, pages 54–59 > Working with Gum Paste, pages 60–63 > Making Basic Figures, pages 68–73

MAKING THE BRIDE'S BODY

3 For the head, form ½ oz. (15g) of flesh-colored paste into a rough almond shape, the narrower end being the chin. Mark the mouth and eyes using the piping tube. Insert a spaghetti strand into the bride's body, then fix the head in place over the spaghetti and secure with edible glue.

4 Make the eyes from a pinch of black paste and attach with edible glue.

5 Make two ears from a pinch of flesh-colored paste rolled into two balls. Indent the ears using the small end of the ball tool and attach to the head with more glue. Add a pinch of flesh-colored paste to the center of the face to form the nose.

2 Make the bust section from ¾ oz. (20 g) of flesh paste, shaping the neck down to the waist, and taking care not to overdo the bust area. Attach to the base over the spaghetti strand using edible glue. Leave to dry.

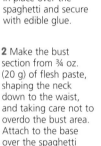

6 Make the arms from ¼ oz. (7 g) of flesh-colored paste. Roll thin, delicate arms, and flatten one end for hands. Attach the arms to the body using edible glue.

7 Make the bride's hair by extruding ¾ oz. (20 g) of the black paste mixed with shortening through the extruder to give strands of paste. Secure these to the head using edible glue.

1 Shape the flower paste into the base of the figure by forming a cone and flattening the top. Insert a spaghetti strand into the top of the cone.

Continued over the page ➡

CLOTHING THE BRIDE

8 Roll out 1 oz. (30 g) of red paste to make the skirt section. Use the exacto knife to trim the skirt to fit around the figure. Emboss the paste using the fabric-effect embossing tool and use the exacto knife to trim the top of the skirt. Fit the skirt around the figure then fix in place with edible glue. Use the exacto knife to trim off the excess neatly at the back, and to trim the base of the skirt.

9 Roll out a small amount of red paste for the bra top. Trim to fit but not too small. Emboss as before and attach to the bust section using edible glue. Trim further if required.

To make the headdress, follow Steps 10–12 opposite.

10 For the long headdress, thinly roll out the remaining red paste and shape into a rectangle. Shape one short end so that it curves naturally around to join the long sides. Drape the headdress over the head and secure with edible glue. Allow to drape onto the floor and trim as required.

11 Use the ribbon cutter to cut a thin, neat strip from the remnants of red paste, to run the full length around the front edge of the headdress. Attach to the front of the headdress using edible glue.

12 Make a gold paint by mixing the gold luster and vodka, and apply to the ribbon with the paintbrush.

13 Using just the gold luster and a clean, dry paintbrush, dust the skirt and bra front to give a golden-red effect.

Continued over the page ➡

MAKING THE GROOM'S BODY

17 Shape the head from ¾ oz. (20 g) of flesh-colored paste. Mark the mouth using the piping tube, and the closed eyes using the flower veining tool. Attach to the body over the spaghetti strand in the neck and secure with edible glue. Position close to the bride's head. Make the groom's hair by extruding the black paste mixed with shortening through the extruder to give strands of paste.

16 Place a small pinch of flesh-colored paste, rolled into a ball, onto the neck section. Secure with edible glue.

18 Before proceeding, make the groom's coat (see Step 19 opposite). Then shape the arms from the remaining flesh-colored paste and attach to the body over the jacket. Then add the hands, made from ¼ oz. (7 g) of flesh paste.

15 Shape the white paste into an oval for the body. Flatten one end and push this end onto the legs, using edible glue to secure. Push a strand of spaghetti into the neck section and leave standing to dry.

14 Roll the cream flower paste into a long, thin sausage for the legs. Use the exacto knife to cut the sausage into two equal lengths, then fix them together with edible glue. Push a small strand of spaghetti into each end of each leg and lay flat to dry.

CLOTHING THE GROOM

20 Use the red paste to shape the turban. Insert the large end of the ball tool to make space for the head, thinning the paste and stretching it. Shape the turban further, using the flower veining tool to indent the folds of fabric. Attach the turban to the head using edible glue.

21 Shape pinches of red paste into a tiny feather shape, and texture the feather with the flower veining tool. Attach to the front of the turban using edible glue.

22 Make a long scarf from ½ oz. (15 g) of red paste. Shape it into a long thin sausage, flatten and roll out thinly. Trim into a neat shape using the pizza wheel. Gather up the scarf, creating folds and creases, using the flower veining tool to assist.

23 Use ¼ oz. (7 g) of red paste for the shoes. Shape two pointed teardrops then roll up the point at the end to make a distinctive shoe shape. Push the shoes onto the spaghetti strands in the legs and fix with edible glue. Stand up and support upright until dry.

19 The groom's coat is made from 2 oz. (60 g) of cream paste. Roll it out fairly thinly and shape into a rectangle using the pizza wheel. Wrap it around the body and secure with edible glue. Join the edges together at the front of the figure and cut away any excess with the exacto knife. Pinch in the paste at shoulder level, cutting off any excess.

24 Use the paintbrush and gold luster to dust the turban, shoes and trousers. Make a paint by mixing the gold powder and vodka, and apply to the scarf with a clean paintbrush.

57 love birds

The bird bride makes a delightful alternative to the traditional bride. Of course the bird bride needs her groom.

Materials	Tools	Colors Used
• Gum paste	• Workboard	**For the bride:**
• Colorings	• Flower veining tool	○ 4 oz. (115 g)
• Cornstarch (for dusting)	• Exacto knife	○ ¼ oz. (7 g)
• Edible glue	• Paintbrush	● Pinch
	• Rolling pin	**For the groom:**
	• Foam pad	○ 3 oz. (90 g)
	• Toothpick	○ ¼ oz. (7 g)
	• Pizza wheel	● Pinch
		● ¾ oz. (20 g)

See also
Designing Your Cake, pages 26–31 > Working with Color, pages 54–59 > Texturing, pages 74–81

FEMALE BIRD　　　　**MALE BIRD**

4 To make the headdress, roll out the remaining white paste to a circle and frill as before. Fold the circle over, but not in half, to create a two-tiered frill. Attach this to the head of the bride using edible glue.

3 Thinly roll out ½ oz. (15 g) of white paste and use the exacto knife to cut out a circle for the train. Press the edge into the foam pad and roll the toothpick over it to give it a frill. Gather the train to a point and attach to the back of the head using edible glue.

2 Shape the yellow paste into a wedge and use the exacto knife to cut through the end to make the beak. Attach the beak to the face using edible glue. Roll tiny amounts of black paste between your fingers to form the eyes and fix in place using edible glue.

5 Shape the yellow paste into a wedge and use the exacto knife to cut through the end to make the beak. Roll two balls from black paste for the eyes.

6 Form the male's body in the same way as the female's (see Step 1).

7 Roll the gray paste out thinly for the jacket. Use the pizza wheel to cut out the jacket shape, then cut the vent in the center back using the exacto knife. Position the jacket on the back of the bird. Secure with edible glue.

8 Make the top hat from remnants of gray paste and attach with edible glue.

1 Form the body, tail and head of the female bird from 3 oz. (90 g) of white paste by shaping it into a rough triangle with rounded corners. Fan out the broad end for the tail and curve it upward. Use the flower veining tool to frill and texture the tail.

58 cuddling teddies

One of these cute bears could be used to decorate a cake for a young child, or they could be dressed up with a top hat and veil as a bride and groom.

Materials

- Gum paste
- Colorings
- Cornstarch (for dusting)
- Dried spaghetti strands
- Edible glue

Tools

- Workboard
- Stitch embossing tool
- Paintbrush
- Exacto knife

Colors Used

- 3¾ oz. (110 g)
- ¼ oz. (7 g)
- Pinch

See also
Designing Your Cake, pages 26–31 > Working with Color, pages 54–59 > Texturing, pages 74–81

3 Shape the head from ½ oz. (15 g) of gray paste. Form the paste into a ball first, then shape slightly into a triangle, broadening the top of the head. Attach the head to the body over the spaghetti strand, using edible glue to secure.

2 Shape two arms from ¾ oz. (20 g) of gray paste. Attach the arms to the bear at the shoulder using edible glue.

4 Fashion two ears from ¼ oz. (7 g) of gray paste. Shape the paste into a ball, then flatten it and use the exacto knife to cut it in half. Shape each ear with the ball tool and attach to the head using edible glue. Use the stitch embossing tool to add more seams as required.

5 Shape a snout from ¼ oz. (7 g) of white paste and attach to the face using edible glue. Add a black nose using a tiny ball of black paste.

6 Make two eyes from more tiny balls of black paste, and fix with more glue.

1 Using 1½ oz. (45 g) of gray paste, mold the body into a rough egg shape, with the base being the broadest part. Push a spaghetti strand through the neck in preparation for supporting the head. Emboss with the stitching tool.

7 Shape two legs from ¾ oz. (20 g) of gray paste. Shape them straight, forming the foot at one end, then cut the other end at an angle using the exacto knife. Place the legs up against the bear's body and secure with edible glue. Make the white bear in exactly the same way.

59 champagne bottle

The perfect topper for a celebration, however wild or sophisticated.

Materials
- Gum paste
- Colorings
- Cornstarch (for dusting)
- Edible glue
- 24 ga. gold wire
- Gold luster
- Silver luster
- Vodka

Tools
- Workboard
- Rolling pin
- Ribbon cutter
- Paintbrush

Colors Used
- 1 oz. (30 g)
- 1 oz. (30 g)
- ½ oz. (15 g)

See also
Designing Your Cake, pages 26–31 > Working with Color, pages 54–59 > Texturing, pages 74–81

5 Make the bubbles from tiny pinches of white paste. Shape into balls. Thread a few onto the wires to give the impression of exploded fizz. Attach the others to the bottle neck.

4 Shape the cork from the remaining cream paste and insert into it a short length of gold wire. Crimp a few more lengths of wire and add these too to suggest movement.

3 Make the foil around the bottle neck in the same way as you did the label (see Step 2).

2 Shape the label from ½ oz. (15 g) of cream paste. Roll thinly before cutting with the ribbon cutter. Attach to the bottle with edible glue.

6 Paint the bubbles with silver paint and the cork and labels with gold paint. Make the paints by mixing the lusters with the vodka (see page 59).

1 Shape the bottle from green paste. Make a sausage shape, thinning out for the neck of the bottle. Flatten both ends. Stand upright and dry.

60 wedding bells

These elegant wedding bells are attached by coiled silver wire and entwined with draped fabric and a few delicate butterflies.

Materials

- Gum paste
- Cornstarch (for dusting)
- Edible glue
- 24 ga. silver wire

Tools

- Workboard
- Wedding bell mold
- Toothpick
- Rolling pin
- Butterfly mold
- Paper
- Pizza wheel
- Flower veining tool
- Paintbrush

Colors Used

○ 4½ oz. (130 g)

See also
Designing Your Cake, pages 26–31 > Working with Color, pages 54–59 > Texturing, pages 74–81

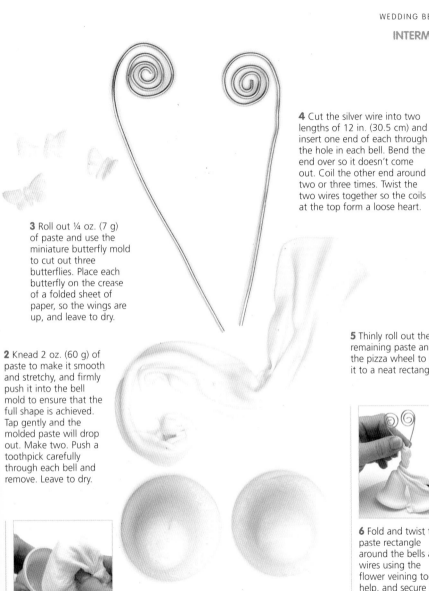

4 Cut the silver wire into two lengths of 12 in. (30.5 cm) and insert one end of each through the hole in each bell. Bend the end over so it doesn't come out. Coil the other end around two or three times. Twist the two wires together so the coils at the top form a loose heart.

3 Roll out ¼ oz. (7 g) of paste and use the miniature butterfly mold to cut out three butterflies. Place each butterfly on the crease of a folded sheet of paper, so the wings are up, and leave to dry.

2 Knead 2 oz. (60 g) of paste to make it smooth and stretchy, and firmly push it into the bell mold to ensure that the full shape is achieved. Tap gently and the molded paste will drop out. Make two. Push a toothpick carefully through each bell and remove. Leave to dry.

5 Thinly roll out the remaining paste and use the pizza wheel to trim it to a neat rectangle.

6 Fold and twist the paste rectangle around the bells and wires using the flower veining tool to help, and secure it to itself using edible glue. Attach the butterflies with edible glue.

1 Dust the inside of the wedding bell mold with cornstarch.

bows

Bows can be added to many other toppers, and here are four different bow designs to choose from. With these toppers you can also experiment with color.

Tools

- Workboard
- Rolling pin
- Ribbon cutter
- Paper towels
- Paintbrush
- Textured rolling pin
- Exacto knife
- Daisy mold
- Toothpick
- Foam pad
- Flower veining tool

CRISSCROSS BOW

1 Roll out the paste on the workboard and use the ribbon cutter to cut out strips about ½ x 2 in. (1.5 x 5 cm).

2 Fold the strips in half over rolled paper towels so they keep their shape as they dry.

3 Make 16 loops. Place 10 loops in a circle as the base layer and secure in place with edible glue. Make a layer of 5 loops on top

and in between the previous layer. Secure with edible glue.

4 Place the final loop on top and secure as before. Leave the paper towels in place until the bow is completely dry.

LOOPED BOW

1 Roll out the red paste using a rolling pin.

2 Texture the paste using the textured rolling pin, rolling both ways to achieve the crisscross effect.

3 Using the ribbon cutter, cut strips of paste. Cut the bow sections together so they are the same length. Fold the strips in half over rolled paper

towels so they keep their shape as they dry.

4 Cut tails into the ends of the ribbons using the exacto knife. Bring them all together and secure using edible glue.

5 Make a ball with the remaining paste and texture it with the textured rolling pin. Use edible glue to secure the ball over all the joins.

Materials	Colors Used
• Gum paste • Colorings • Cornstarch (for dusting) • Edible glue	● 3 oz. (90 g)

Materials	Colors Used
• Gum paste • Colorings • Cornstarch (for dusting) • Edible glue	● 4 oz. (115 g)

See also
Designing Your Cake, pages 26–31 > Working with Color, pages 54–59 > Texturing, pages 74–81

ROSETTE

1 Roll out the blue paste. Use the ribbon cutter to cut 12 strips about ¾ in. (2 cm) wide.

2 Fold the strips in half—from the outside of one end to the inside of the other. Secure with edible glue.

3 Attach six strips on the base layer, securing with edible glue. Attach a further six on top.

4 Put the remaining paste into a daisy mold and secure the shape to the center of the bow with edible glue.

FRILLY BOW

1 Roll out the yellow paste into a long strip then use the ribbon cutter to cut a strip about 1 in. (2.5 cm) wide.

2 Frill each edge of the yellow paste with a toothpick on a foam pad.

3 Make two bow loops using 2 in. (5 cm) for each loop. Support the loop with paper towel until dry. Use remnants of the frilled paste to make two tails for the bow.

4 Make thin strips of yellow and green paste to decorate the loops; attach with edible glue.

5 Bring all four ends together in the center and use the remaining yellow paste to create a knot. Secure in place using edible glue.

Materials	Colors Used
• Gum paste	● 4 oz. (115 g)
• Colorings	
• Cornstarch (for dusting)	
• Edible glue	

Materials	Colors Used
• Gum paste	○ 2 oz. (60 g)
• Colorings	● 1 oz. (15 g)
• Cornstarch (for dusting)	
• Edible glue	

new baby

This sweet collection of toppers, all with a baby theme, could be grouped together to make a cute cake to celebrate a new baby. Use pale pink or another color if desired.

Tools

- Workboard
- Toothpicks
- Rolling pin
- Pizza wheel
- Flower veining tool
- Butterfly cutter
- Paper towel
- Exacto knife
- Foam pad
- Quilting tool
- Paintbrush
- Medium and small circle cutters

FOOTPRINTS

1 Use 1 oz. (30 g) of pale blue paste for each footprint. Pinch off a small part for the toes, then shape the rest into an oval.

2 Use your fingers to indent the paste for the arch of the foot.

3 Make the toes using the remnants of the paste.

Materials	Colors Used
• Gum paste	2 oz. (60 g)
• Coloring	
• Cornstarch (for dusting)	
• Edible glue	

BABY BOTTLES

1 Make each bottle from 2 oz. (60 g) of white paste. Mold into a cone-like shape but with a flattened end, and pinch the base to sharpen the edge.

2 Shape a collar from colored paste.

3 Use 1 oz. (30 g) of white paste for each nipple. To shape the nipples, start with a fat sausage shape and slim the center. Use a toothpick to indent a hole in the top of the nipple.

Materials	Colors Used
• Gum paste (with added gumtex)	6 oz. (170 g)
• Colorings	½ oz. (15 g)
• Cornstarch (for dusting)	½ oz. (15 g)
• Edible glue	

See also
Designing Your Cake, pages 26–31 > Working with Color, pages 54–59 > Texturing, pages 74–81

BIB

1 Roll the white paste out and use the pizza wheel to cut the bib into a circle.

2 Use the wheel to cut out the neck area of the bib.

3 Use the flower veining tool to texture the bib with crisscross lines.

4 Use the butterfly cutter to indent the paste and leave the butterfly outline behind. Place a paper towel behind the bib to support it until dry.

5 Roll out the remnants of white paste and use the exacto knife to cut out a strip 1 in. (2.5 cm) wide. Place the strip on the foam pad and use a toothpick to frill the edge.

6 Attach the frilled strip to the edge of the bib using edible glue, and use the quilting tool to texture the join.

7 Make ties from the yellow paste. Attach with edible glue.

PACIFIER

1 Mold the white paste into a nipple shape and place to one side.

2 Take 2 oz. (60 g) of pale navy paste and roll it out thickly. Use the medium circle cutter to cut out the first circle, then use the small cutter to cut a smaller circle from the center to make the ring.

3 Pinch off a small amount from the remaining blue paste and put to one side.

Thickly roll out what is left and cut another large circle. Soften the edges using the flower veining tool.

4 Use edible glue to attach the nipple to one side of the circle and the ring to the other. Use the remaining blue paste to make a tie and fix to the back of the base.

Materials	Colors Used
• Gum paste	3½ oz. (105 g)
• Colorings	½ oz. (15 g)
• Cornstarch (for dusting)	
• Edible glue	

Materials	Colors Used
• Gum paste	1 oz. (30 g)
• Colorings	3 oz. (90 g)
• Cornstarch (for dusting)	
• Edible glue	

69 rag doll

A charming rag doll would be perfect for any little girl's cake.

Materials	Tools	Colors Used
• Gum paste	• Workboard	○ 10 oz. (300 g)
• Colorings	• Flower veining tool	● 2 oz. (60 g)
• Cornstarch (for	• Paintbrush	1¾ oz. (50 g)
dusting)	• Exacto knife	1½ oz. (45 g)
• Dried spaghetti	• Rolling pin	● Pinch
strands	• Textured rolling pin	2½ oz. (75 g)
• Edible glue	• Pizza wheel	● ¼ oz. (7 g)
• Shortening	• Foam pad	
	• Toothpick	
	• Quilting tool	
	• Paper towel	
	• Extruder with	
	multihole disk	

See also
Designing Your Cake, pages 26–31 > Working with Color, pages 54–59 > Making Basic Figures, pages 68–73

MAKING THE BODY

2 Make an oval-shaped head from 1 oz. (30 g) of flesh-colored paste, but pinch a little off for the nose and cheeks. Indent a mouth into a grin with the flower veining tool. Don't attach the head until you have clothed the doll (see Steps 6–13 over the page).

3 Shape two blobs of black paste into eyes and attach to the face with edible glue. Make a slightly larger blob of flesh-colored paste for the nose and attach. Flatten two balls of pink paste and fix to the face as cheeks.

4 Roll 1 oz. (30 g) of dark pink paste with 1 oz. (30 g) of white paste into a sausage shape to make the striped effect for the legs. Use the exacto knife to cut the sausage in half. Attach the legs to the base of the body with more glue. Bend one leg up.

1 Make a body shape from 2 oz. (60 g) of white paste. Sit the body upright and push three dried spaghetti strands through the body, leaving around ⅜ in. (1 cm) protruding to support the head.

5 Using 1 oz. (30 g) of dark pink paste, make two shoes. Fix the shoes in place with edible glue.

Continued over the page ➡

CLOTHING AND ACCESSORIES

6 To make the dress, thinly roll out 4 oz. (115 g) of white paste into a circle shape and texture with the textured rolling pin. Trim the edges with the pizza wheel.

7 Drape the dress over the body, allowing the spaghetti to pierce through it.

8 Use 2 oz. (60 g) of white paste and roll it into a sausage. Roll thinly with the rolling pin and cut out a strip that is 1 in. (2.5 cm) wide. Place the strip on the foam pad and "frill" all the way along the end of the paste using a toothpick.

9 Attach the frill to the bottom of the dress, using the quilting tool to texture as you go.

11 Shape the hands from ½ oz. (15 g) of flesh-colored paste and attach them to the ends of the arms with the glue.

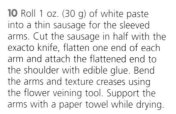

10 Roll 1 oz. (30 g) of white paste into a thin sausage for the sleeved arms. Cut the sausage in half with the exacto knife, flatten one end of each arm and attach the flattened end to the shoulder with edible glue. Bend the arms and texture creases using the flower veining tool. Support the arms with a paper towel while drying.

12 Roll out the yellow paste and use the exacto knife to cut out the jacket. Place the jacket over the dress, around the sleeves.

13 Cut out a collar and attach with edible glue. Make three buttons and fix them to the front of the jacket with more glue.

14 Mix shortening with the orange paste until it is very soft. Extrude the paste through the extruder to make the hair. Make long lengths for the bunches, pinch in where the bows will be attached, then cut lengths short for the bangs area. Attach to the doll with edible glue.

15 Make two bows by shaping two balls of green paste into teardrops. Draw the flower veining tool down the shape to indent. Then attach to the hair with edible glue. Add two tails and a small ball of paste to cover any joins.

70 clown

This clown looks rather silly with his bright red nose and mouth, not to mention his clothes! You can make your clown as bright as you like.

Materials

- Gum paste
- Colorings
- Cornstarch (for dusting)
- Edible glue
- Dried spaghetti strands

Tools

- Workboard
- Exacto knife
- Flower veining tool
- Paintbrush
- Small blossom cutter (plunger)
- Rolling pin
- Pizza wheel

Colors Used

- 2 oz. (60 g)
- 3 oz. (90 g)
- 4 oz. (115 g)
- 1 oz. (30 g)
- 2 oz. (60 g)
- ¼ oz. (7 g)
- 2 oz. (60 g)
- 1 oz. (30 g)

See also
Designing Your Cake, pages 26–31 > Working with Color, pages 54–59 > Making Basic Figures, pages 68–73

MAKING THE BODY

4 Make the body from 3 oz. (90 g) of orange paste. Make it as broad as the pants top. Mark down the center using the flower veining tool and attach to the figure. Push two strands of spaghetti through the neck and body into the legs, to support.

5 Roll the remaining orange paste into a sausage shape and cut in half to make the arms. Flatten one end and attach this end to the shoulders using edible glue. Bend the arms and use the flower veining tool to crease the elbows. Support the arms in this position until dry.

6 Make the hands and cuffs from ¾ oz. (20 g) of white paste and fix to the arms with more glue.

3 Shape the navy paste into a rough rectangle for the pants. Cut into one side slightly with the exacto knife to make the pants—quite short. Use the flower veining tool to make creases around the legs. Broaden the top of the pants.

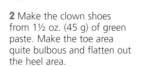

2 Make the clown shoes from 1½ oz. (45 g) of green paste. Make the toe area quite bulbous and flatten out the heel area.

1 Edible glue and dried spaghetti strands are used in this model to attach the pieces together and add strength, so make sure you have some to hand before you begin.

Continued over the page →

MAKING THE HEAD AND FACIAL FEATURES

9 For the eyes, roll remnant pieces of white, navy and black paste into balls—large white balls, medium blue balls and small black balls—and flatten. Fix in place directly above the nose.

10 Make large and small balls from the orange paste and attach to the head for the hair, working around the ears and around the back of the head. Manipulate the paste using the flower veining tool to give a curly, frizzy look.

8 Use the ball tool to indent the ears and attach to sides of head with edible glue.

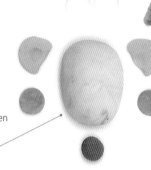

7 Pinch off a little flesh paste for the two ears, then shape 2 oz. (60 g) of the flesh paste into a large head and attach to the neck, over the spaghetti.

11 Make two large balls from remnants of orange paste, then flatten and attach to the face for the cheeks.

12 Make a semicircle to surround the mouth from ¼ oz. (7 g) of white paste.

13 Make the nose and mouth from ½ oz. (15 g) of pink paste. Roll the paste in the palm of your hand to achieve the shape of the lips. Indent the lip line using the flower veining tool.

ADDING DETAILS

15 Use the blossom cutter to cut out three green blossoms for the hat, with white centers, and one pink blossom for the shoe, with a white center.

14 Make the hat from 1½ oz. (45 g) of pink paste, having already pinched off a tiny amount to make one blossom. Roll the paste out thinly and use the exacto knife to cut out a circle for the brim, then use the rest to make the hat. Fix the two elements together with edible glue, then attach the hat to the head using a strand of dried spaghetti.

16 Make two teardrop shapes from green paste and indent them using the flower veining tool. Use edible glue to fix the two points together on the body and attach a ball of green paste over the top.

18 Thinly roll out the yellow paste and cut out two suspenders using the pizza wheel. Attach to the pants front using edible glue, pass the suspenders over the shoulders and fix again at the pants back.

17 To make colorful buttons, form pinches of paste into balls, flatten them and indent them twice with the end of the dried spaghetti. Attach to the figure with edible glue.

71 open anniversary book

This book can be made as large or as small as required for the top of the cake and can have inscriptions written on the pages.

Materials	Tools
• Gum paste	• Workboard
• Colorings	• Rolling pin
• Cornstarch (for dusting)	• Exacto knife or kemper knife
• Edible glue	• Flower veining tool
	• Toothpick or strand of dried spaghetti
	• Pizza wheel

Colors Used

- 2 oz. (60 g)
- 4 oz. (115 g)
- 1 oz. (30 g)

See also
Designing Your Cake, pages 26–31 > Working with Color, pages 54–59 > Texturing, pages 74–81

EASY

3 Use the flower veining tool to mark the center of the pages, and press firmly to make a curved shape in the center.

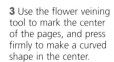

4 Mark the pages using the exacto knife blade, along all sides.

2 Roll the ivory paste into a slightly smaller rectangle and soften the edges. Using an exacto knife or Kemper knife, cut the rectangle into a parallelogram by trimming off the two short sides at an angle, as an open book would be shaped.

5 Use the exacto knife blade to "cut" some of the page corners so they can be curved upward using a toothpick or strand of spaghetti, to make them look dog-eared.

1 Roll the dark brown paste into a rectangle 5 x 3 in. (12.5 x 7.5 cm) for the book binding. Soften the corners.

6 Roll a rectangle of dark yellow paste. Cut a strip from it using the pizza wheel to make the bookmark. Use an exacto knife blade to cut the fringe. Place the bookmark over the center of the book and secure with edible glue.

72 trophy

Wrap any color of ribbon around this trophy and celebrate with your favorite football or baseball team.

Materials

- Gum paste
- Cornstarch (for dusting)
- Edible glue
- Royal icing
- Dried spaghetti strands
- Gold or silver luster
- Vodka

Tools

- Workboard
- Rolling pin
- Extra large, small and extra small circle cutters
- Paintbrush
- Ribbon cutter
- Paper towel

Colors Used

- 5 oz. (140 g)

See also
Designing Your Cake, pages 26–31 > Working with Color, pages 54–59 > Texturing, pages 74–81

4 For the trophy body shape 2 oz. (60 g) of paste into a cylinder, then narrow one end. Attach to the base by threading a spaghetti strand through the trophy body and stem and down to the base.

5 To make the trophy lid, cut out another small circle from the white paste and place on top of the trophy body, securing with edible glue. Shape ½ oz. (15 g) of paste into a hemisphere and attach to the circle with edible glue. Add a knob to the top.

3 For the trophy stem, roll ½ oz. (15 g) of paste very thinly and wrap around a spaghetti strand. Secure to the base of the trophy with edible glue.

6 Roll the remaining paste quite thinly, to ⅛ in. (2.5 mm), and use the ribbon cutter to cut strips for the trophy handles. Curl one end of the handle one way and the other end the opposite way. Attach to the trophy with edible glue, and support the shape with a paper towel until dry.

2 Make a ball from ½ oz. (15 g) of paste and flatten to a hemisphere, but keep as much height as possible. Place this centrally on the top disk and secure with royal icing.

1 Roll 1 oz. (30 g) of paste. Use the circle cutters to cut out one large, one medium and one small circle. Pile up the three circles in size order, with the largest at the bottom. Fix with edible glue.

7 Make a paint by mixing gold or silver luster with vodka, and paint the cup.

swimmer

This is a really cunning cake topper that rises cleverly out of the cake.

Materials

- Gum paste
- Colorings
- Cornstarch (for dusting)
- Edible glue
- Blue and white royal icing
- Piping gel (optional)

Tools

- Workboard
- Ball tool
- Paintbrush
- Rolling pin
- Exacto knife
- Paper towel
- Flower veining tool

Colors Used

- 6 oz. (170 g)
- ¾ oz. (20 g)
- ¼ oz. (7 g)
- Pinch

See also
Designing Your Cake, pages 26–31 > Working with Color, pages 54–59 > Texturing, pages 74–81

5 Shape the arm from 2 oz. (60 g) of flesh-colored paste. Start with a sausage shape, then work down shaping the upper arm and elbow and using the flower veining tool to add texture. Thin down the forearm, pinching in slightly at the wrist. Cut the fingers, making sure the thumb is nearest the head when attached to the body.

6 Place the body up against the head. Place a paper towel over the swimmer's head (see page 69), then drape the arm over this, keeping the elbow bent and the fingers just touching the surface.

7 Smooth the paste of the arm and body to join the two together. Indent the armpit with the large end of the ball tool. Use the flower veining tool to add creases to the neck.

4 Shape the body from 2 oz. (60 g) of flesh-colored paste. Don't worry about the base of the shape too much since you can cover this with the cake topping.

3 Roll out the purple paste thinly and drape over the head for the swimming cap. Secure in place using edible glue. Trim away the excess with an exacto knife and tuck the ends under the head.

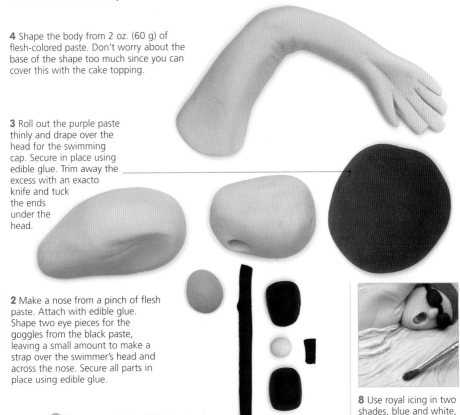

2 Make a nose from a pinch of flesh paste. Attach with edible glue. Shape two eye pieces for the goggles from the black paste, leaving a small amount to make a strap over the swimmer's head and across the nose. Secure all parts in place using edible glue.

1 Use 2 oz. (60 g) of flesh-colored paste to shape the head into a teardrop. Use the ball tool to shape an open mouth and elongate by pushing up and down and backward into the head. Insert a pinch of pink paste into the mouth and use the ball tool to push into place.

8 Use royal icing in two shades, blue and white, to create the water surface, and work this around the swimmer, imagining where the ripples would be. Alternatively, use piping gel to make the water look wet.

74 doctor

A slightly disheveled and very busy doctor, standing still for just a moment. This is a really special cake topper since the features of the doctor can be changed to look just like your special doc.

Materials

- Gum paste
- Flower paste
- Colorings
- Cornstarch (for dusting)
- Dried spaghetti strands
- Shortening
- Edible glue
- Silver luster powder
- Vodka

Tools

- Workboard
- Flower veining tool
- Paintbrush
- Exacto knife
- Extruder with multihole disk
- Ball tool
- Quilting tool

Colors Used

Gum paste:
- ● 2 oz. (60 g)
- ○ 2 oz. (60 g)
- ● ¼ oz. (7 g)
- 1¾ oz. (50 g)
- ● ¼ oz. (7 g)
- 1 oz. (30 g)

Flower paste:
- ● 1 oz. (30 g)

See also
Designing Your Cake, pages 26–31 > Working with Color, pages 54–59 > Making Basic Figures, pages 68–73

MAKING THE BODY

4 Shape three-quarters of the flesh-colored paste into a sphere for the head and attach to the body.

5 Before proceeding with Steps 5 and 6, make the doctor's jacket (see Steps 10–12 over the page). Now make the arms and hands. Roll ¼ oz. (7 g) of white paste into a long sausage and cut in half. Bend them slightly and use the flower veining tool to put elbow creases on the sleeve. Flatten one end and attach this to the jacket using edible glue.

3 Make a body shape from 1¾ oz. (50 g) of yellow paste. Sit the body upright and push a strand of spaghetti into the neck end, leaving a little protruding to support the head. Attach to the legs.

6 Make two hands from ½ oz. (15 g) of flesh paste. Shape the fingers using the flower veining tool. Attach to the ends of the sleeves.

1 Make two sausage shapes for the legs with the black flower paste, making them fatter at one end than the other. Use the flower veining tool to texture this fat end, putting creases into the pant bottoms. Push a small strand of spaghetti into each end of each leg.

2 Use ¼ oz. (7 g) of black paste for each of the shoes, shaped into teardrops. Push the shoes onto the spaghetti strands in the legs and fix with edible glue. Stand the model up to dry, making sure the piece is straight.

Continued over the page →

ADDING DETAILS

7 Roll a pinch of black paste into two small balls for the eyes and a pinch of flesh-colored paste into a ball for the nose.

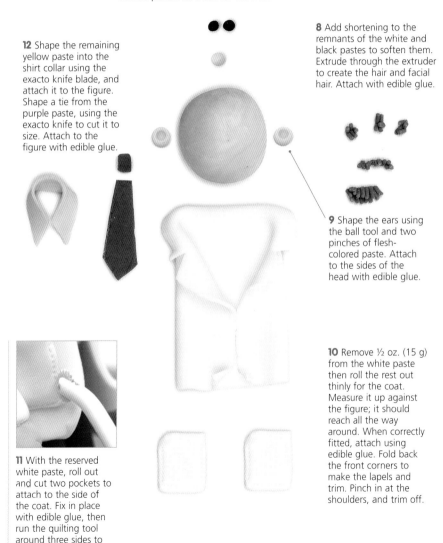

12 Shape the remaining yellow paste into the shirt collar using the exacto knife blade, and attach it to the figure. Shape a tie from the purple paste, using the exacto knife to cut it to size. Attach to the figure with edible glue.

8 Add shortening to the remnants of the white and black pastes to soften them. Extrude through the extruder to create the hair and facial hair. Attach with edible glue.

9 Shape the ears using the ball tool and two pinches of flesh-colored paste. Attach to the sides of the head with edible glue.

10 Remove ½ oz. (15 g) from the white paste then roll the rest out thinly for the coat. Measure it up against the figure; it should reach all the way around. When correctly fitted, attach using edible glue. Fold back the front corners to make the lapels and trim. Pinch in at the shoulders, and trim off.

11 With the reserved white paste, roll out and cut two pockets to attach to the side of the coat. Fix in place with edible glue, then run the quilting tool around three sides to simulate stitching.

13 Roll the remaining black paste thinly and cut to create the stethoscope. Paint the ends of the stethoscope with the silver luster powder mixed with vodka and drape around the neck.

14 Make a roll of paper to stick out from the doc's pocket using ¼ oz. (7 g) of beige paste. Roll out thinly, cut and trim, then roll up.

15 Use the remaining beige paste to make the book cover; fill with "pages" and secure together. Stuff the book and roll of paper into the pockets of the coat, securing with edible glue.

musical notes

This collection of easy-to-make toppers is perfect for anyone who plays or is learning to play a musical instrument.

Tools

- Workboard
- Rolling pin
- Exacto knife
- Template card, pencil and scissors (optional)
- Extruder with large single-hole disk
- Paintbrush
- Black edible-ink pen
- Ruler

75 EIGHTH NOTE

1 Roll the paste out quite thickly.

2 Using the exacto knife, and a template if preferred (see page 250), cut out the shape of the eighth note.

3 Leave to dry on a flat surface.

Materials	Colors Used
• Gum paste • Colorings • Cornstarch (for dusting)	● ½ oz. (15 g)

76 TREBLE CLEF

1 Soften the paste using shortening and extrude through the extruder into a long string.

2 Wrap the string into the shape of the treble clef. Where the string crosses itself, use edible glue to secure in place.

3 Leave to dry on a flat surface for 48 hours before handling.

Materials	Colors Used
• Gum paste • Colorings • Cornstarch (for dusting) • Shortening • Edible glue	● ½ oz. (15 g)

See also
Designing Your Cake, pages 26–31 > Working with Color, pages 54–59 > Templates, pages 250–251

QUARTER NOTE

1 Roll the paste out thickly.

2 Using the exacto knife, and a template if preferred (see page 250), cut out the shape of the quarter note.

3 Leave to dry on a flat surface.

4 Make a paint using silver dusting powder and vodka and use a paintbrush to apply it to the note.

MUSIC PARCHMENT

1 Roll out the paste very thinly into a rectangle.

2 Use the paintbrush to curl up the short ends of the rectangle, making one slightly off angle.

3 Use the exacto knife to cut into the parchment slightly and to age it.

4 Use the paintbrush to apply gold dusting powder around the edges of the parchment to age it further.

5 When dry, use black edible ink pen and a ruler to draw musical staves onto the parchment.

Materials	Colors Used
• Gum paste • Colorings • Cornstarch (for dusting) • Silver dusting powder • Vodka	● ½ oz. (15 g)

Materials	Colors Used
• Gum paste • Colorings • Cornstarch (for dusting) • Gold dusting powder	● ¼ oz. (7 g)

camping

This is a great topper for a cub scout, or could form its own mini cake.

Materials

- Gum paste
- Colorings
- Cornstarch (for dusting)
- Edible glue
- Vodka
- Shortening

Tools

- Workboard
- Paste smoother
- Exacto knife
- Rolling pin
- Paintbrush
- Toothpick
- Extruder with single-hole disk

Colors Used

- 7 oz. (200 g)
- ½ oz. (15 g)

See also
Designing Your Cake, pages 26–31 > Working with Color, pages 54–59 > Texturing, pages 74–81

2 Roll 3½ oz. (105 g) green paste out to make a large rectangle, large enough to cover both sides of the tent, billow out at the back and protrude over the front. Cut with the exacto knife. Curve one short end of the paste to form the back of the tent. Lay this shape over the tent and attach with edible glue. Tweak out the back to give a smooth shape.

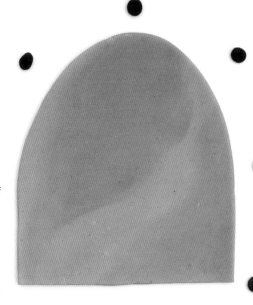

3 Use balls of black paste for tent pegs, and attach with edible glue.

4 Trim off one end of a toothpick. "Wash" the toothpick with vodka and allow to dry, then insert it at the front of the tent as the tent support. Cover the top with a cone of green paste.

5 Roll out ½ oz. (15 g) of green paste to make three ventilation flaps. Attach with edible glue.

1 Mold 3 oz. (90 g) of green paste into a prism. Use the paste smoother to assist in achieving a smooth triangular shape with a pointed peak. If necessary, use the exacto knife to sharpen the shape.

6 Make ropes by extruding black paste through the single-hole disk in the extruder, having softened the paste first using shortening. Form ropes reaching from the supports to the ground.

pond life

Collected together on one cake, these toppers would make a fantastic pond scene.

Tools

- Workboard
- Rolling pin
- Paintbrush
- Exacto knife
- Flower veining tool
- Extruder with single-hole disk
- 24 ga. wire
- Stem tape
- Rose petal cutter
- Foam pad
- Bone tool

80

DRAGONFLY

1 Roll out 1¾ oz. (50 g) of paste, broad at one end, thin at the other. Push a spaghetti strand into the broad end.

2 Roll the remaining paste into a ball and attach to the broad end of the sausage with edible glue.

3 Paint the tail blue and the body and head black.

4 Make two slits using the exacto knife just behind the head for the wings.

5 Cut two wings from gelatin sheets and insert into the slits.

Materials	Colors Used
• Gum paste • Cornstarch (for dusting) • Dried spaghetti strand • Blue and black paste colors • Edible glue • Gelatin sheets	2 oz. (60 g)

81

LILYPAD

1 Roll out the paste quite thinly and cut out a rough circle using an exacto knife.

2 Cut out a triangle shape from the circle and soften the edges so that they curve.

3 Create the veins of the lilypad using the flower veining tool.

4 Dust the pad with deep and light green dusting powders to add shadows.

Materials	Colors Used
• Gum paste • Coloring • Cornstarch (for dusting) • Deep and light green dusting powders	2 oz. (60 g)

See also
Designing Your Cake, pages 26–31 > Working with Color, pages 54–59 > Texturing, pages 74–81

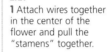

LILY

1 Attach wires together in the center of the flower and pull the "stamens" together.

2 Dampen the "stamens" with edible glue and dip in stem tape.

3 Roll out the paste quite thinly, then cut out three petals using the rose petal cutter or exacto knife blade. Insert a wire up the center of the petal.

4 Place the petals on the foam pad and use the end of the rolling pin to soften the edges a little.

5 Use the bone tool to soften the edges and make them curvy, then use the flower veining tool to indent a crease down the center of each petal. Pinch a point lightly at the tip.

6 Attach these three petals to the flower center with stem tape.

7 Follow Steps 3–5 to make five more petals, and attach these to the bud as the second row.

8 Use a paintbrush to dust the petals with pink dusting powder, to give depth and interest to the display.

BULRUSHES

1 Mix shortening with brown flower paste to soften it, then extrude through the extruder to make the stalks of the bulrushes. Use the exacto knife to cut the stalks to varying lengths.

2 Roll out the brown paste and shape into tiny rectangles using the exacto knife. Add a touch of edible glue, then wrap the paste around the bulrush stalks near the top,

leaving ⅛ in. (2.5 mm) of stalk protruding above. Trim off excess brown paste using the exacto knife.

3 Roll the green paste out thickly, and use the exacto knife to cut out long triangular shapes. Soften the edges, then run the flower veining tool up the center. Bend each leaf inward, then attach to the base of the bulrushes using edible glue.

Materials	Colors Used
• Gum paste • Flower paste • Colorings • Cornstarch (for dusting) • Shortening • Edible glue	Gum paste: ¾ oz. (20 g) ¼ oz. (7 g) Flower paste: ¾ oz. (20 g)

Materials	Colors Used
• Gum paste • Colorings • Cornstarch (for dusting) • Edible glue • Pink dusting powder	1 oz. (30 g)

gardening set

These items will make a fabulous cake topper for a green-fingered friend. You can make the plant pots different sizes, or, if a particularly large pot is required, use the watering can method.

Tools

- Workboard
- Rolling pin
- Circle cutter (any size)
- Pizza wheel
- Paintbrush
- Exacto knife
- Ribbon cutter
- Foam pad
- Piping tube
- Scissors
- Ball tool

Materials

- Gum paste
- Colorings
- Cornstarch (for dusting)
- Edible glue

Colors Used

● 4 oz. (115 g)

84

WATERING CAN

1 Roll out ¼ oz. (7 g) of green paste, and use the circle cutter to cut out the base of the watering can.

2 Roll 1½ oz. (45 g) paste out, then use the pizza wheel to cut out a rectangle with the long edges measuring the same as the circumference of the circle cut in Step 1. Attach the rectangle to the circle base using edible glue. The paste will hold itself upright while you coil the body around the base. Leave to dry.

3 Roll out ¼ oz. (7 g) of green paste and cut out another circle. Use the circle cutter to cut a segment of paste away from the initial circle. Attach this piece to the top of the watering can using edible glue. Allow the lid to "dome." Leave to dry.

4 Make the spout using ¼ oz. (7 g) green paste. Roll it into a long sausage shape. Use the exacto knife to cut one end flat and the other end at an angle. Roll out ¼ oz. (7 g) of green paste to make a long sausage, then flatten it and roll it thinly. Use the ribbon cutter to cut out a long green ribbon. Attach the spout to the can using edible glue, holding it in place with a foam pad, then wrap the green ribbon around the spout and fix it to the watering can with edible glue. Trim the ribbon as necessary.

5 Make handles using the ribbon cutter as you did in Step 4. Attach using edible glue. Make rivets for joins from small balls of paste. Emboss them with the pointed end of the piping tube.

See also
Designing Your Cake, pages 26–31 > Working with Color, pages 54–59 > Texturing, pages 74–81

85

PLANT POT

1 Thinly roll out 1 oz. (30 g) of orange paste. Use the pizza wheel to cut out a small rectangle. Wrap this around the upturned piping tube, keeping the base edge of the paste flat, and pinch the ends together. Use scissors to cut off the excess; neaten the join.

2 Use the exacto knife to neaten the top edge.

3 Take the piping tube out, turn the pot the right way up and drop a ball of paste into the pot for the base. Use the ball tool to squash the base piece into place.

4 Use the remaining paste to make a band around the top of the pot.

86

SPADE

1 Roll brown paste into a sausage. Thin out and trim the ends. Push a strand of spaghetti into each end.

2 Roll a smaller sausage to make the top handle. Cut and trim to fit, then push onto the top of the shaft.

3 Roll the white paste into a square. Cut out the spade shape, thinning the blade end.

4 Attach the blade to the handle, covering the join with a thin, neat strip of white paste.

5 Paint the blade silver using silver luster powder mixed with vodka.

Materials	Colors Used
• Gum paste	⬤ 2 oz. (60 g)
• Colorings	
• Cornstarch (for dusting)	
• Edible glue	

Materials	Colors Used
• Gum paste	⚪ 1 oz. (30 g)
• Colorings	⬤ 1 oz. (30 g)
• Cornstarch	
• Dried spaghetti strand	
• Silver luster powder	
• Vodka	

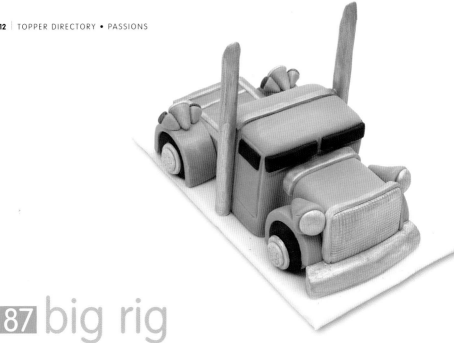

87 big rig

Like the train on page 216, this big rig can be designed to fill the whole of the cake top.

Materials

- Gum paste
- Flower paste
- Fondant
- Colorings
- Cornstarch (for dusting)
- Edible glue
- Royal icing
- Silver luster powder
- Vodka

Tools

- Workboard
- Cake card: 10 x 4 in. (25 x 10 cm)
- Three polystyrene blocks: 4 x 3 x 2 in. (10 x 7.5 x 5 cm); 2 x 3 x 2 in. (5 x 7.5 x 5 cm); 1½ x 3 x 4 in. (3.5 x 7.5 x 10 cm)
- Paintbrushes
- Rolling pin
- Exacto knife
- Flower veining tool
- Medium and small circle cutters
- Ribbon cutter
- Textured rolling pin
- Kemper knife
- Two cake smoothers

Colors Used

Gum paste:
- 9 oz. (255 g)
- 4 oz. (115 g)
- 3 oz. (90 g)

Flower paste:
- 3 oz. (90 g)

Fondant:
- 3 oz. (90 g)

See also
Designing Your Cake, pages 26–31 > Working with Color, pages 54–59 > Texturing, pages 74–81

BASIC BUILDING BLOCKS

3 Position all three orange blocks on the prepared cake card and secure with royal icing.

4 Indent door and window frames using the flower veining tool.

2 Cover three polystyrene blocks with orange gum paste. Roll out the paste to a depth of ¼ in. (5 mm). Paint the polystyrene blocks with edible glue then use the rolling pin to help position the paste over the blocks. Cut off excess paste using the exacto knife.

5 Shape four wheels from 3 oz. (90 g) of black paste and score the tire tread with the exacto knife. Flatten the tires, place them against the rig. Secure with royal icing.

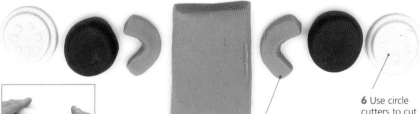

1 Cover the cake card with the white fondant and leave to dry.

7 Roll out the remaining orange paste to a thickness of ¼ in. (5 mm) and cut mudguards for the wheels using the ribbon cutter. Cut into 2½ in. (6 cm) lengths and drape over the wheels.

6 Use circle cutters to cut medium and small circles of white paste and attach to the wheels with more royal icing.

Continued over the page →

ADDING DETAILS

9 Roll 1 oz. (30 g) of black paste thinly and use the ribbon cutter to cut windows for the windscreen and doors. Secure in place using edible glue.

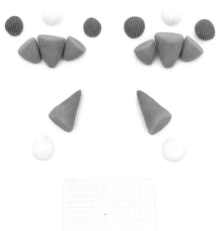

8 Use the remaining orange paste to shape two large, two medium and four small cones for lights. Attach these to the mudguards using royal icing, with the large at the front and one medium and two small on each back wheel. Make headlights from small pinches of white and red paste and secure in place using edible glue.

10 To make the grille, roll out 1 oz. (30 g) of white paste quite thinly and texture with the textured rolling pin by rolling in one direction then turning 90 degrees and rolling again to give the grille effect. Shape into a rectangle using the Kemper knife. Attach to the front of the big rig using edible glue.

11 To mold the front and back bumpers, shape the white gum paste into two long rectangles. Curve one around the front of the big rig and one around the back.

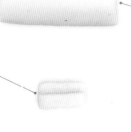

12 For the doorstep, use ¼ oz. (7 g) white paste. Shape into a rectangle and, using an exacto knife, cut another rectangle from this rectangle to fit the step below the door. Attach to the rig with edible glue.

13 Roll ¼ oz. (7 g) white paste thinly, cut into ribbons using the ribbon cutter and use appropriate lengths to finish off the hood, roof, wheeltrim, and flatbed. Secure in place using edible glue.

14 Make the exhaust chimneys from white flower paste. Roll it into a long length using two cake smoothers, then cut into two sections at an angle using the exacto knife. Trim to the same length and leave to dry. Secure in place using royal icing.

15 Make a silver paint by mixing silver luster powder with vodka and use this to paint the rig. Leave to dry.

88 train

This train could be designed to fill the whole of the cake top, or as a mini version accompanied by other birthday-boy treats.

Materials

- Gum paste
- Colorings
- Cornstarch (for dusting)
- Edible glue
- Dried spaghetti strands

Tools

- Workboard
- Rolling pin
- Exacto knife
- Paintbrush
- Flower veining tool
- Medium circle cutter
- Small circle cutter
- Small square cutter

Colors Used

- 1 oz. (30 g)
- 6½ oz. (185 g)
- ½ oz. (15 g)
- ½ oz. (15 g)
- 3 oz. (90 g)
- 3¼ oz. (93 g)

See also

Designing Your Cake, pages 26–31 > Working with Color, pages 54–59 > Texturing, pages 74–81

6 Mold 1 oz. (30 g) of black paste into the front buffer by shaping a triangle and softening the edges. Use the flower veining tool to texture the top and secure with edible glue.

7 Make a funnel from purple paste. Attach to the boiler using spaghetti and edible glue. Shape a smaller funnel from red paste.

5 Roll out the remnants of blue paste and use the exacto knife to cut a thin strip that tapers out at one end. Fix the strip along one side with edible glue.

4 Shape the yellow paste into a domed front for the boiler, and attach with edible glue.

8 Roll out the remaining black paste. Use the circle cutter to cut out circles, then cut centers out using a smaller circle cutter. Cut the discarded small circles into cross shapes for the wheel spokes. Attach using edible glue. When dry, place the wheels up against the train bed and secure in place with edible glue. Cut out two drive arms the same length as the train bed. Leave to dry. Attach to the wheels with edible glue.

3 Shape the remaining green paste into a cylinder for the boiler. This should be 1 in. (2.5 cm) shorter than the train bed. Position in place.

2 Shape 3 oz. (90 g) of green paste into a rectangular block. This will support the train bed and give the necessary height so that the wheels can stand upright. Place under the train bed.

1 Make the train bed first by rolling out the blue paste into a rectangle, then trim using the exacto knife. Lie flat to dry.

9 Thinly roll out the red paste. Use the exacto knife to cut out a square for the roof and two rectangles. Cut one window from each rectangle, then trim off ¼ in. (5 mm) from the width but only 1 in. (2.5 cm) in length to form the cab. Cut a third rectangle with a window cutout only, for the front of the cab. Leave to dry. Secure in place on the train using edible glue. Hold in place until set, then attach the roof with more glue.

89 tractor

The tractor is a tricky cake topper, but your hard work will definitely pay off. Change the colors if you like, but for best effects use strong primary colors like red and yellow.

Materials	Tools
• Gum paste	• Workboard
• Colorings	• Rolling pin
• Cornstarch (for dusting)	• Paintbrush
• Edible glue	• Exacto knife
• Shortening	• Flower veining tool
• Dried spaghetti strands	• Circle cutters, two large sizes and one small
	• Extruder with large and medium single-hole disks
	• Textured rolling pin
	• Ball tool

Colors Used

● 11 oz. (310 g)
● 7 oz. (200 g)
◐ 2¾ oz. (82 g)

See also
Designing Your Cake, pages 26–31 > Working with Color, pages 54–59 > Texturing, pages 74–81

STRUCTURING THE TRACTOR

2 Roll out 1 oz. (30 g) of red paste. Cover the front 1 in. (2.5 cm) of the tractor. Secure with edible glue. Trim with the exacto knife. Roll out 1 oz. (30 g) of red paste and cover another 2½ in. (6.5 cm) along the tractor, ¾ in. (2 cm) down each side.

3 Shape the front wheels from 1 oz. (30 g) of black paste. Texture the tread into the wheel using the pointed end of the flower veining tool by pressing it firmly into the paste at an angle.

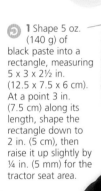

1 Shape 5 oz. (140 g) of black paste into a rectangle, measuring 5 x 3 x 2½ in. (12.5 x 7.5 x 6 cm). At a point 3 in. (7.5 cm) along its length, shape the rectangle down to 2 in. (5 cm), then raise it up slightly by ¼ in. (5 mm) for the tractor seat area.

4 Use circle cutters to cut large and small circles of yellow paste to finish the wheels. Secure in place using edible glue.

6 Make the back wheels from 3 oz. (90 g) of black paste. Shape into two large wheels, measuring 2½ in. (6 cm) in diameter. Fashion smaller yellow circles for the inner wheel, as in Step 4. Position the block from Step 1 against the tractor engine and attach the wheels.

5 Make a third pad of red paste, measuring 1 oz. (30 g), as you did in Step 2. Shape this into a rectangle measuring 2½ x 1¼ in. (6 x 3 cm). Curve one end and place at the engine end of the tractor hood.

Continued over the page ➡

ADDING DETAILS

7 Soften 1 oz. (30 g) of red paste using shortening and extrude through the extruder with the large single hole. Do the same with ¾ oz. (20 g) yellow paste. Attach the red string over the end of the tractor and around the tractor hood section and down toward the seat area.

8 Cut out the radiator grille from 1 oz. (30 g) of black paste. Texture the grille using the textured rolling pin, rolling it both ways to give a crisscross pattern. Attach to the tractor with edible glue. Attach the yellow strand from Step 7 around the radiator grille and around the tractor hood.

11 Shape the bumper from 1 oz. (30 g) of black paste. Roll into a sausage, flatten the ends, and angle using the flower veining tool. Position on the tractor and smooth.

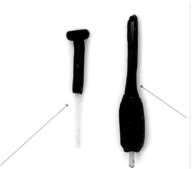

10 Shape a gearshift by wrapping a small stick of spaghetti with remnants of black paste. Add a small ball on top and push into the tractor at the seated area.

9 Cover a spaghetti strand, which should be 2½ in. (6.5 cm) long, with a thin layer of black paste, then re-cover 1 in. (2.5 cm) to give the fatter section. Trim off a little from the bottom of the strand then push this into the tractor hood.

12 Cut two ¾ x 3¾ in. (2 x 9.5 cm) rectangles from red paste and drape over the back wheels. Support the back part of the mudguard until dry.

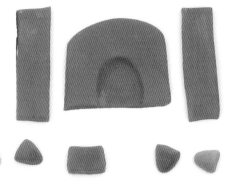

13 Roll out 2 oz. (60 g) of red paste quite thickly into a rectangle of 2½ x 2 in. (6.5 x 5 cm). Trim with the exacto knife, curving one long side slightly—the back of the seating area. Indent the seat area using the large end of the ball tool. Make a small backrest from a pinch of red paste. Position over the back section of the tractor.

14 Shape the back lights from remnants of paste. Add a little black paste to the remaining yellow to give an orange paste for the lights. Secure with edible glue.

handbags and shoes

Any girl would be delighted with these toppers on her cake.

Tools

- Workboard
- Rolling pin
- Flower veining tool
- Paintbrush
- Exacto knife
- Stitching tool
- Small blossom cutter
- Cone tool

GREEN SAC AND CLOGS

1 Put aside ½ oz. (15 g) of the leaf green paste for the clogs.

2 Roll 5 oz. (140 g) of paste into a rough circle, leaving it quite thick.

3 Bring the edges together and pinch in the "neck" of the sac. Use the flower veining tool to tweak and define the top of the bag.

4 Roll ¼ oz. (7 g) of paste into a sausage shape and wrap this around the sac neck. Texture the tie with the flower veining tool. Make two tassels for the front and attach with edible glue.

5 Shape each clog from half of the put-aside green paste. Make the sole first, and make the heel section deeper. Cut out the upper of the clog, a semicircular shape, with the exacto knife, and attach using edible glue. Run the stitching tool around the front of the clogs.

Materials

- Gum paste
- Colorings
- Cornstarch (for dusting)
- Edible glue

Colors Used

- 5¾ oz. (163 g)

See also
Designing Your Cake, pages 26–31 > Working with Color, pages 54–59 > Texturing, pages 74–81

BLACK BAG AND SANDALS

1 Put aside 1½ oz. (45 g) of black paste.

2 Shape 1½ oz. (45 g) of black paste into a tall rectangle, measuring 2½ x 2 x ¼ in. (6 x 5 x 0.5 cm). Flatten the ends to make the shape more rounded.

3 Use the exacto knife to cut a strip of the printed fondant sheet and secure with edible glue around the bag.

4 Cut a thick strip of black paste using the exacto knife to wrap around the base and top of the bag, covering over the ends of the printed sheet.

5 Roll out the remaining paste and cut long straps for the bag approximately ¼ x 2 in. (0.5 x 5 cm). Emboss both sides of the strap using the stitching tool.

6 Cut one strap to fasten the bag closed, then two for handles. Secure with edible glue.

7 Make fasteners for the straps from black paste remnants, and attach with edible glue. Mix silver luster powder with vodka and paint the fasteners with the resulting silver paint.

8 Divide the put-aside paste in half, pinch off a

little for the straps, and shape the rest into two platform shoes. Attach the straps with edible glue, then use the blossom cutter to cut out three flowers for each shoe from the printed fondant sheet.

Materials

- Gum paste
- Colorings
- Cornstarch (for dusting)
- Edible glue
- Printed fondant
- Silver luster powder
- Vodka

Colors Used

- ○ 1 oz. (30 g)
- ● 3 oz. (90 g)

Continued over the page ➔

PINK BAG AND FLIP-FLOPS

1 Mold 1½ oz. (45 g) of dark pink paste into a rough house shape.

2 Roll out 1 oz. (30 g) of dark pink paste very thinly, then use the flower veining tool to texture creases. Gather up the paste to accentuate the creases.

3 Use the exacto knife to trim the textured paste into two neat rectangles, and attach to each end of the bag using edible glue. Trim away the excess paste.

4 Cut a small rectangle to cover the top of the bag, like a lid. Emboss the edge with the stitching tool and attach to the bag as before.

5 Shape a ball fastener and attach to the bag, then emboss with the cone tool. Mix gold luster with vodka and paint the fastener with the resulting gold paint.

6 Use the remnants of paste to make the handle. Emboss around the edge as before. Secure to bag with edible glue, supporting the center if required.

7 Shape two flip-flop shapes from the shades of light pink paste. Make straps, attach with edible glue and decorate with balls of pink paste.

Materials

- Gum paste
- Colorings
- Cornstarch (for dusting)
- Edible glue
- Gold luster
- Vodka

Colors Used

- 3 oz. (90 g)
- 1 oz. (30 g)

See also
Designing Your Cake, pages 26–31 > Working with Color, pages 54–59 > Texturing, pages 74–81

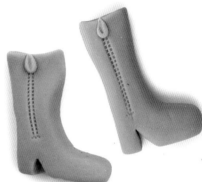

93

PINK BAG AND BOOTS

1 Put aside 3 oz. (90 g) of dull pink paste.

2 Shape 3 oz. (90 g) of the paste into a box shape measuring 2¾ x 1¼ x 1½ in. (7 x 3 x 4 cm). Soften the edges.

3 Use the flower veining tool to emboss the top of the bag for the opening. Use the stitching tool on either side of the opening to suggest a zipper.

4 Shape more of the paste into a zipper tab. Make two front pockets from pinches of paste shaped into squares. Attach with edible glue.

5 Make pocket flaps by rolling out small amounts of paste and cutting to shape with the exacto knife. Emboss the edges with the stitching tool. Add a tiny triangle as a fastener and secure all elements with edible glue.

6 Make tiny side pockets in the same way, but smaller.

7 Roll out a sausage shape from ¾ oz. (20 g) of paste. Fix with edible glue around the edges of the bag to neaten and accentuate the bag shape.

8 Roll out more of the paste and use the exacto knife to cut two long, quite thick straps. Attach to the bag using edible glue, then use the stitching tool to imprint a cross on each to fasten to the bag.

9 Divide the put-aside 3 oz. (90 g) of paste in two for the boots. Shape each into a sausage, then bend one short end by 90 degrees.

10 Shape the short end into the shoe, giving a heel and smoothing the top. Shape the rest into the long boot, with the top fatter than the ankle section.

11 Use the stitching and flower veining tools to mark the zipper of the boot. Shape more of the paste into tiny zipper tabs.

Materials

- Gum paste
- Colorings
- Cornstarch (for dusting)
- Edible glue

Colors Used

● 10¼ oz. (305 g)

94 alien

The basic shapes of this alien can be rearranged to create your own variation.

Materials

- Gum paste
- Colorings
- Cornstarch (for dusting)
- Edible glue
- Dried spaghetti strands
- 22 ga. wire

Tools

- Workboard
- Flower veining tool
- Paintbrush
- Ball tool
- Rolling pin
- Exacto knife

Colors Used

6½ oz. (185 g)
¼ oz. (7 g)
Pinch
¼ oz. (7 g)
¼ oz. (7 g)

See also
Designing Your Cake, pages 26–31 > Working with Color, pages 54–59 > Texturing, pages 74–81

4 Make the arms in the same way as the neck, but use two strands of 22 ga. wire to support them. Attach one end of each arm at the head, and allow the long arm to trail on the ground. Add the claws, fixing with edible glue.

5 Add more yellow balls for the eye stalks, pushing a strand of spaghetti through them to secure. Fix two white balls on the ends and attach two black pupils with edible glue.

6 Roll out the green paste thinly and use the exacto knife to cut a long strip for the tongue. Attach one end in the mouth with edible glue, and roll the other end up and secure to the body. Add black dots to the tongue with more glue.

3 Insert two spaghetti strands 2 in. (5 cm) in length into the body as support for the neck. Push various sized balls of yellow paste down the strands to form the neck. Leave a small amount of spaghetti protruding to support the head. Support the neck in place until set. Make a ball for the head from ¾ oz. (20 g) of yellow paste. Secure this over the protruding spaghetti while still supporting the neck in its upright position. Use the ball tool to indent the mouth.

7 Roll out the red paste and use the exacto knife to cut out shapes to decorate the body. Fix using edible glue.

2 Shape 1½ oz. (45 g) of yellow paste into a squat ball. Secure on top of the heels of the feet with edible glue.

1 Shape ¾ oz. (20 g) of yellow paste into two triangles and soften the edges. Use the flower veining tool to indent alien toes.

95 mermaid

A little experience is required to make this figure, but have a go; at least there are no legs or feet to fiddle with.

Materials

- Gum paste
- Fondant
- Colorings
- Cornstarch (for dusting)
- Edible glue
- Dried spaghetti strands
- Shortening
- Dusting powder

Tools

- Workboard
- Horseshoe tool
- Exacto knife
- Paintbrush
- Piping tube
- Rolling pin
- Flower veining tool
- Extruder with multihole disk

Colors Used

Gum paste:
- 4 oz. (115 g)
- 3 oz. (90 g)
- 1 oz. (30 g)
- Pinch

Fondant:
- 2 oz. (60 g)

See also
Designing Your Cake, pages 26–31 > Working with Color, pages 54–59 > Making Basic Figures, pages 68–73

4 Shape the body from 1½ oz. (45 g) of flesh-colored paste and attach onto the fish tail using a dot of edible glue and a spaghetti strand. Push a strand of spaghetti through the neck section ready for the head.

5 Shape the head from ½ oz. (15 g) of flesh paste. Make the nose and ears from tiny balls of flesh paste and fix in place with edible glue. Indent the mouth using the broad end of the piping tube and indent the eye sockets using the pointed end. Use a pinch of black paste to make two small balls for the eyes.

6 Roll out the remaining blue paste, and cut out the bodice shape using the exacto knife. Attach to the body using edible glue and tweak into place using the flower veining tool.

3 Use the smaller end of the horseshoe tool to emboss sections of the tail to create a fish-scale pattern. Split the end of the tail using the exacto knife.

7 Shape the arms from the remaining flesh-colored paste and attach to the body using edible glue.

2 Using three-quarters of the blue paste, form the tail. Use your fingers to create a tapered fin shape.

8 Make hair from the green paste. Work shortening into the paste to soften it, then extrude it through the extruder. Attach the strands to the head using edible glue. Lightly dust the hair with disco green dusting powder.

1 Make a rock shape from yellow fondant and leave to dry. This will be the seat for your mermaid.

9 Sit the mermaid on the rock and push a spaghetti strand through the center of the body and through the rock shape. Use the flower veining tool to crease the top of the legs.

96 pirate

This rather wizened old sea dog has led a tumultuous life at sea, losing his leg, hand and eye in the process.

Materials	Tools
• Gum paste	• Workboard
• Colorings	• Exacto knife
• Cornstarch (for dusting)	• Paintbrush
• Dried spaghetti strands	• Flower veining tool
• Edible glue	• Ball tool
• Wooden skewer	• Rolling pin
• Silver luster powder	
• Vodka	

Colors Used

- 1 oz. (30 g)
- 2 oz. (60 g)
- 5½ oz. (155 g)
- 4 oz. (115 g)
- ½ oz. (15 g)
- 1½ oz. (45 g)
- 6½ oz. (185 g)
- ½ oz. (15 g)

See also
Designing Your Cake, pages 26–31 > Working with Color, pages 54–59 > Making Basic Figures, pages 68–73

MAKING THE BODY

3 Shape the body from 2 oz. (60 g) of flesh-colored paste. Push two strands of dried spaghetti through the neck area, ready to support the head.

4 Before proceeding with this step, make the pirate's jacket (see Steps 17–18 on page 233). Now make the arms. Roll out 1 oz. (30 g) of purple paste into a sausage shape for the arms. Cut the sausage in half and flatten one end of each arm. Use edible glue to attach the flattened end of each arm to the shoulders. Use the flower veining tool to add creases. Support the arms in place while drying.

2 Use the exacto knife to cut a cube of brown for the pants. Shape further with your fingers.

5 Support the wrist sections by adding cuffs of the remaining yellow paste, ¼ in. (5 mm) in width. Attach over part of the wrist and the jacket sleeve.

1 Shape one boot from ¾ oz. (20 g) of black paste. Push two strands of dried spaghetti into the boot, allowing them to protrude ⅜ in. (1 cm).

6 Shape one hand and one hook from ¾ oz. (20 g) of flesh-colored paste. Attach to the arms with edible glue and leave supported in place while drying. Paint the hook with silver paste, made by mixing the silver luster powder with vodka.

8 Attach the boot and the wooden leg to the pants using edible glue. Lay down until set, then stand up. Push a strand of spaghetti through the pants to support the body.

7 Use a wooden skewer to make the wooden leg. Measure it up against the boot so the skewer is the same length, then cover the skewer in edible glue. Roll out the brown paste and cover the skewer, cutting off the excess. Leave to dry.

Continued over the page ➡

MAKING THE HEAD

10 Make a large bulbous nose with a wart on from ¼ oz. (7 g) of flesh paste, and attach to the face with edible glue.

11 Use more flesh paste to make two large ears. Indent each with the ball tool and attach to each side of the head.

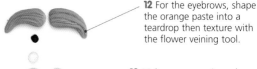

12 For the eyebrows, shape the orange paste into a teardrop then texture with the flower veining tool.

13 Make one eye using a large ball of flesh paste. Score it with the exacto knife blade but don't cut all the way through. Attach this to the face with more glue. Push a little white paste into the slit, and top this with a dot of black paste. For the second eye, use a small ball of flesh paste, flatten it and attach to the face. Curve the eyebrows around the eyes and secure in place with edible glue.

9 Shape 2½ oz. (75 g) of flesh paste into an oval and attach to the body over the spaghetti. Use the exacto knife to form an opening for the mouth, and open it slightly with the flower veining tool. Poke in a wedge of pink paste and smooth it off.

14 Shape and texture the mustache pieces in the same way as the eyebrows. Attach to the face below the nose, slightly covering the mouth.

15 Roll remnants of white paste into a small, short sausage shape. Use the exacto knife blade to mark out teeth, then use the flower veining tool to indent further. Cut to fit and attach to the top and bottom of the mouth.

16 Cut the beard from orange paste in two sections Use the exacto knife to sharpen the ends of the beard. Fix in place when you have finished the jacket and embellishments.

ADDING DETAILS

20 Use the purple paste to shape a hat. Form a sausage shape first, then mold it into a triangular shape to drape over the sides of the head. Attach in the usual way.

21 Make and flatten a small ball of black paste for the eye patch. Fix with edible glue over the closed eye. Make the strings by rolling a little of the paste between two palms, and attach to the patch and the head.

19 Make the skull and crossbones by cutting out a circle from the white paste remnants, trim by one-third and, on the flat side, use the flower veining tool to indent twice, thus creating the skull. Use the same tool to make two eye sockets. Cut out two thin strips of white paste and attach to the hat (see Step 20), crossing over, then place the skull shape over the join. Make eight tiny balls to put at each end of the strips to look like bone ends.

17 Roll 2 oz. (60 g) of dark purple paste into a rectangle for the jacket. Wrap it around the body, meeting at the front. Trim the corners from the bottom. Pinch the paste together at the shoulders and trim with the exacto knife.

18 Roll out the yellow paste into a strip about ⅛ in. (2.5 mm) wide. Cut two lengths about 1 in. (2.5 cm) long and place them across the upper body with edible glue. Make four small balls and attach them to each end of the strips. Cut two more lengths about ¼ in. (5 mm) long and put aside. Cut a buckle using the exacto knife and fix to the front of the jacket. Attach the two short strips vertically underneath the buckle.

97 fairy

Combine this fairy with the pixie on page 236 and the fairytale castle on page 242 for the ultimate fantasy-themed cake.

Materials

- Gum paste
- Colorings
- Cornstarch (for dusting)
- Edible glue
- Dried spaghetti strands
- Gelatin leaves

Tools

- Workboard
- Flower veining tool
- Horseshoe tool
- Piping tube
- Paintbrush
- Exacto knife
- Rolling pin
- Leaf cutter

Colors Used

- ○ 3½ oz. (100 g)
- ● 2¼ oz. (65 g)
- ● 2 oz. (60 g)

See also
Designing Your Cake, pages 26–31 > Working with Color, pages 54–59 > Making Basic Figures, pages 68–73

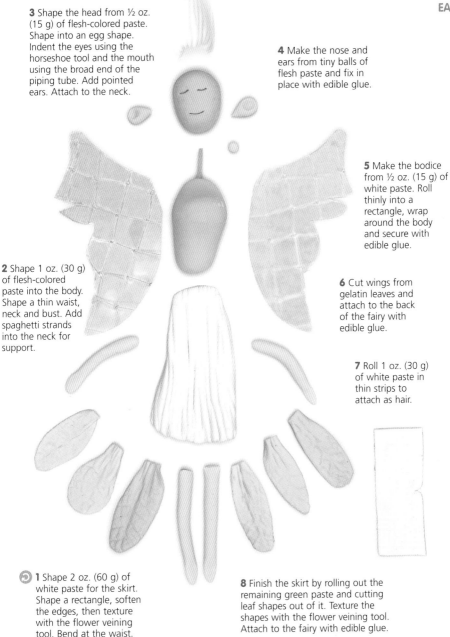

3 Shape the head from ½ oz. (15 g) of flesh-colored paste. Shape into an egg shape. Indent the eyes using the horseshoe tool and the mouth using the broad end of the piping tube. Add pointed ears. Attach to the neck.

4 Make the nose and ears from tiny balls of flesh paste and fix in place with edible glue.

5 Make the bodice from ½ oz. (15 g) of white paste. Roll thinly into a rectangle, wrap around the body and secure with edible glue.

2 Shape 1 oz. (30 g) of flesh-colored paste into the body. Shape a thin waist, neck and bust. Add spaghetti strands into the neck for support.

6 Cut wings from gelatin leaves and attach to the back of the fairy with edible glue.

7 Roll 1 oz. (30 g) of white paste in thin strips to attach as hair.

1 Shape 2 oz. (60 g) of white paste for the skirt. Shape a rectangle, soften the edges, then texture with the flower veining tool. Bend at the waist.

8 Finish the skirt by rolling out the remaining green paste and cutting leaf shapes out of it. Texture the shapes with the flower veining tool. Attach to the fairy with edible glue.

98 pixie

Cute and easy to make, this pixie would look great holding hands with the fairy on page 234.

Materials

- Gum paste
- Colorings
- Cornstarch (for dusting)
- Edible glue
- Dried spaghetti strands
- Shortening

Tools

- Workboard
- Rolling pin
- Exacto knife
- Paintbrush
- Flower veining tool
- Ball tool
- Star cutter
- Extruder with multihole disk

Colors Used

- 2¾ oz. (82 g)
- 1 oz. (30 g)
- 1¾ oz. (50 g)
- 3 oz. (90 g)
- Pinch
- ½ oz. (15 g)

See also
Designing Your Cake, pages 26–31 > Working with Color, pages 54–59 > Making Basic Figures, pages 68–73

6 Make pointed ears from ¼ oz. (7 g) of flesh-colored paste. Shape into a teardrop, then indent using the ball tool. Attach to the head using edible glue.

5 Make the hands from ¾ oz. (20 g) of flesh-colored paste and fix to the arms with edible glue.

4 Shape the head from ¾ oz. (20 g) of flesh paste. Open the mouth using the flower veining tool. Mark the eyes.

3 Shape the arms from ½ oz. (15 g) of red paste, in long triangles. Attach one point of the triangle to the shoulder using edible glue.

2 Shape the body from 2 oz. (60 g) of red paste, in a rounded triangle shape. Sit it on top of the pants and secure with edible glue. Push a spaghetti strand into the neck ready for the head.

1 Roll 1 oz. (30 g) of red and 1 oz. (30 g) of white paste into sausages. Then roll them together to form stripy legs. Divide into two and bend to drape over the side of the cake.

7 Roll ½ oz. (15 g) of green paste and cut out a star. Thread the star over the spaghetti strand and over the shoulders. Attach the head.

8 Use 1 oz. (30 g) of green paste to shape the hat. Start with a triangle, elongate it and bend over the point. Use the flower veining tool to add creases. Attach to the head.

9 Make the eyes with a pinch of black paste and attach with glue.

10 Add shortening to the orange paste and extrude through the extruder to make the hair. Attach to the head using edible glue.

11 Shape the shoes from the remaining green paste. Shape a teardrop, then curl the point up. Attach a tiny ball of red paste to each shoe and to the point of the hat.

12 Attach the shoes to the legs using a strand of dried spaghetti.

99 fairy house

These little houses, combined with the pixie on page 236, will make a perfect themed birthday cake, and are very simple to make in less than an hour. Any birthday boy or girl will be thrilled.

Materials	Tools
• Gum paste	• Workboard
• Colorings	• Straight-bladed
• Cornstarch (for dusting)	sharp knife
• Paintbrush	
• Dried spaghetti strands	• Small rolling pin
• Edible glue	• Exacto knife

Colors Used

● 4¼ oz. (122 g)
○ 2½ oz. (75 g)
  ¾ oz. (20 g)
● ½ oz. (15 g)

See also
Designing Your Cake, pages 26–31 > Working with Color, pages 54–59 > Texturing, pages 74–81

2 Shape the red paste into an oval "roof" with a flat base. Set the roof to one side to firm up. Make varying sizes of white balls, flatten, then secure to the roof with edible glue. Brush the roof with edible glue on the flat edge, and place on top of the stem.

3 Roll half the black paste into a sausage and push a strand of spaghetti through the center to give it strength. Leave a short length poking out both ends. Position the chimney on the roof. Shape the remaining black into a semicircle for the "hat" on the chimney and place on top.

1 Roll 2 oz. (60 g) of white into a sausage shape to make the stem. Cut the ends to make a flat top and bottom. Insert a dried spaghetti strand into the stem. Leave to dry for half an hour.

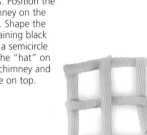

6 Use the remaining white paste to make steps. Make one large rectangle with softened edges and one smaller rectangle to sit on top.

5 Roll the remaining yellow paste into a rectangle for the door. Curve one end. Attach to the white stalk, and trim.

4 Roll half the yellow paste thinly. Use the exacto knife to cut thin strips to make the window frame. You need six short strips for each window: four to make the outer frame and two crossed over to create the panes. Secure onto the house with edible glue.

dragon

This cheerful, colorful dragon is suitable for a young child's birthday cake. He's quite fiddly to make, but the results are well worth it.

Materials

- Gum paste
- Colorings
- Cornstarch (for dusting)
- Edible glue
- Dried spaghetti strands
- Shortening

Tools

- Workboard
- Flower veining tool
- Bone tool
- Exacto knife
- Paper towels
- Paintbrush
- Extruder with multihole disk
- Rolling pin
- Wing template

Colors Used

- 5½ oz. (155 g)
- 2 oz. (60 g)
- ¼ oz. (7 g)
- ¼ oz. (7 g)
- ¾ oz. (20 g)
- ¾ oz. (20 g)

See also
Designing Your Cake, pages 26–31 > Working with Color, pages 54–59 > Texturing pages 74–81

4 Shape the ears from ¼ oz. (7 g) of green paste. Make a triangle. Curl the edges in using the flower veining tool. Secure to the head with edible glue.

5 Make two white eyeballs and two black pupils, and fix in place on the dragon's face with more glue.

6 The dragon's hair is made from yellow and green paste mixed with shortening and extruded through the extruder. Attach the hair to the head using edible glue.

3 Mold the head into a sausage using 1 oz. (30 g) of green paste. Narrow the section between the two ends. Indent the eye sockets and nostrils using the small end of the bone tool. Cut the mouth using the exacto knife and insert a folded paper towel into the mouth to keep it open until dry. When dry, attach the head to the body.

7 Shape the chest section from ¾ oz. (20 g) of orange paste. Make five sausage shapes, with the length getting smaller each time. Flatten the shapes with the rolling pin, then attach to the body using edible glue.

2 For the feet, divide ¾ oz. (20 g) of green paste into two equal pieces and shape each into a teardrop. Texture the toes by indenting using the sharper end of the flower veining tool. Tuck the narrow ends under the body.

8 The wings are made from ¾ oz. (20 g) of orange paste. Roll out the paste on a dusted surface, then cut out the wing shape using the exacto knife. Accentuate the points of the wings with your fingers, pinching the edges together. Support the wings with paper towels while drying. When dry, fix to the dragon's back.

1 Form the body from 3 oz. (90 g) of green paste, tapering the paste to the end of the tail. Narrow the paste to form the neck. Insert two strands of dried spaghetti into the neck, leaving ¼ in. (5 mm) protruding to support the head.

9 Shape the spines from remnants of the orange paste, and attach to the back and tail using edible glue.

10 Make different-shaped dots from the pink paste and secure to the dragon with glue.

101 fairytale castle

A fairytale castle sitting on a hill could be made even more special with the addition of the fairy on page 234.

Materials
- Gum paste
- Fondant
- Colorings
- Cornstarch (for dusting)
- Dried spaghetti strands
- Edible glue

Tools
- Workboard
- Cake smoother
- Exacto knife
- Flower veining tool
- Paintbrush

Colors Used

Gum paste:
- 5 oz. (140 g)
- 2 oz. (60 g)

Fondant:
- 6 oz. (170 g)

See also
Designing Your Cake, pages 26–31 > Working with Color, pages 54–59 > Texturing, pages 74–81

3 Lay each tower down to indent the front, using the flower veining tool to make window slits. Leave the towers to dry lying down and completely flat so they dry straight.

4 Make the roofs from the dark pink paste, fitting them to the towers over the spaghetti while still soft, so they fit together smoothly.

5 Starting with the gate towers, carefully insert the towers into the fondant base, squashing more of the fondant into nooks and crannies to secure. Allow the towers to lean out slightly. Leave to dry.

2 Insert a strand of dried spaghetti into the top of each tower to secure the roofs.

1 Make the towers by rolling 4¼ oz. (120 g) of light pink paste between the workboard and the cake smoother. The towers should vary in height and girth.

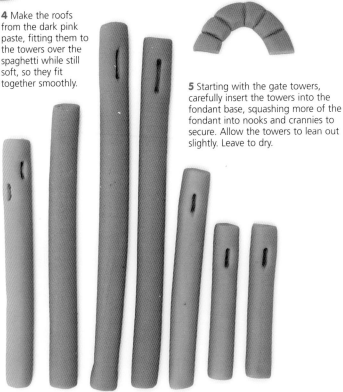

7 Shape the green fondant into a pyramid. On the front face, flatten a ledge and paint with edible glue. Position the towers and, using your fingers, manipulate the green fondant around the base of each tower to secure it.

6 Make the gatehouse arch using ¾ oz. (20 g) of the light pink paste. Shape the paste into a rectangle. Curve the rectangle into an arch shape, then mark the stones using the flower veining tool. Attach to the front of the two gatehouse towers with edible glue.

102 wizard

A benevolent wizard who won't scare anyone,
but nevertheless a charming topper to make.

Materials

- Gum paste
- Colorings
- Cornstarch (for dusting)
- Dried spaghetti strands
- Edible glue
- Shortening
- 24 ga. wire
- ¼ in. (5 mm) width stem tape
- Silver luster powder
- Vodka

Tools

- Workboard
- Rolling pin
- Pizza wheel
- Paintbrush
- Flower veining tool
- Exacto knife
- Extruder with single-hole disk
- Small star cutter

Colors Used

- 5¼ oz. (145 g)
- 2½ oz. (75 g)
- Pinch
- 1 oz. (30 g)
- ½ oz. (15 g)
- 1 oz. (30 g)
- 3 oz. (90 g)

See also
Designing Your Cake, pages 26–31 > Working with Color, pages 54–59 > Making Basic Figures, pages 68–73

MAKING THE BODY

3 Shape the head, nose and ears from 2 oz. (60 g) of flesh paste, and attach the nose and ears using edible glue. Mark the mouth with the sharp end of the flower veining tool. Place the head on top of the body.

4 Use a pinch of black paste to make two tiny eyes and attach to the head using edible glue.

2 Roll out 1½ oz. (45 g) of purple paste. Use the pizza wheel to trim the "fabric" to a long rectangle. Wrap the rectangle around the bottom section of the wizard, securing with edible glue. Use the flower veining tool to make pleats. Cut off excess paste with the exacto knife. Do the same for the top section of wizard using 1 oz. (30 g) of purple paste; however, make this paste thinner. Attach as before.

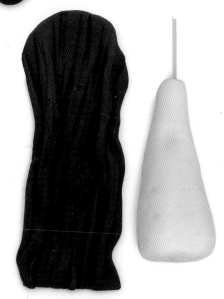

5 Shape the arms from 1 oz. (30 g) of purple paste and attach to the shoulders using edible glue. Push a short length of spaghetti into each end of the arms ready to support the hands. Support the arms in an upright position until secure. Shape two hands from the flesh paste and use the flower veining tool and exacto knife to form thumbs and fingers. Attach the hands to the arms, pushing them onto the spaghetti strands, using edible glue to help. Position the left hand with the palm facing up and the right hand with the palm facing the body.

1 Shape 3 oz. (90 g) of cream paste into a conical shape, but with a flattened top. Push one spaghetti strand through the shape leaving ⅜ in. (1 cm) protruding to support the head. Pinch the shape in at waist level.

Continued over the page ➡

ADDING DETAILS

7 Shape the gold paste into a rough triangle for the shawl and texture with the flower veining tool. Pinch the corners of the shawl and drape it over the wizard's shoulders and down his front, securing with edible glue.

8 Roll ¼ oz. (7 g) of red paste into a thin sausage shape, then flatten in sections to create a scarf to drape along the edges of the shawl, over the wizard's shoulders. Trim off the excess and keep for later.

6 To make the sleeve drapes, roll 1 oz. (30 g) of purple paste into a small rectangle. Texture with the flower veining tool as you did for the robes, then trim to a neat rectangle again. Pinch the two short sides together and loop round, joining two pinched ends together. Flatten and neaten these then thread the arms through the loop. Attach to the shoulders using edible glue.

9 Shape an elongated triangle from the white paste for the beard. Texture with the flower veining tool, trim to fit the face and secure to the face and body with edible glue. Use the flower veining tool to help the paste to stick around the mouth. Use cut-off pieces of white paste to make the mustache, eyebrows and sideburns, again using the flower veining tool to texture.

11 Soften the remaining red paste with shortening and extrude through the extruder to form a string of paste. Wrap the string around the hat and secure in place with edible glue.

10 Shape the remaining purple paste into a wizard's hat and attach to the head using edible glue. Support in place until secure, as it might try to slip off.

12 With any remaining paste, cut out as many stars as possible, and secure them to various parts of the hat, and to the ends of the wizard's scarf.

13 With the remaining white paste, shape an orb for the wizard to hold, and secure in place with edible glue.

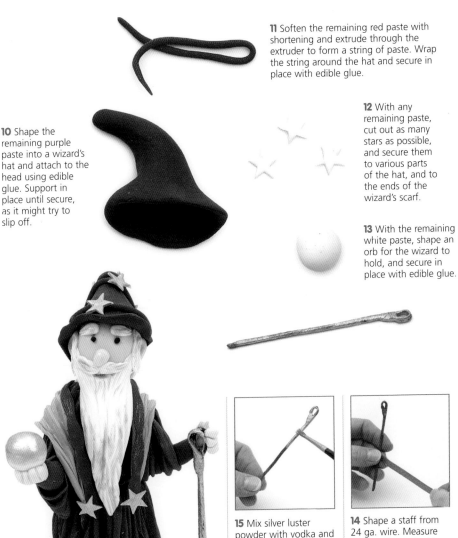

15 Mix silver luster powder with vodka and paint the staff, beard and orb with the resulting silver paint.

14 Shape a staff from 24 ga. wire. Measure the length required to reach the right hand, double this, then tape both lengths of wire together with stem tape. Bend over the top of the staff.

103 crown

This is the perfect topper for the most important person in your household.

Materials

- Gum paste
- Fondant
- Colorings
- Cornstarch (for dusting)
- Edible glue
- Shortening
- Dried spaghetti strands
- Gold luster powder
- Vodka

Tools

- Workboard
- Rolling pin
- Exacto knife
- Paintbrush
- Large pearl mold
- Flower veining tool

Colors Used

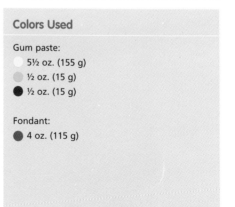

Gum paste:
- 5½ oz. (155 g)
- ½ oz. (15 g)
- ½ oz. (15 g)

Fondant:
- 4 oz. (115 g)

See also
Designing Your Cake, pages 26–31 > Working with Color, pages 54–59 > Texturing, pages 74–81

Make the central design for the crown by shaping a small amount of paste into a ball and a teardrop. Run a spaghetti strand through them with a little protruding from the base of the ball ready for attachment.

Shape the purple fondant to fit in the center of the crown, then, using the flower veining tool, texture and emboss the paste to give a folded fabric effect.

Attach a few cut-off pearls to the points of the crown with more glue.

Soften 2 oz. (60 g) of yellow paste with shortening, then extrude through the extruder. Using edible glue, line the top and bottom edges of the crown with the resulting strings of paste.

Place a strip of paste in the pearl mold and shape a ring of "pearls." Using the exacto knife, trim the back of the pearls, then attach this side around the base of the crown with edible glue.

7 Shape the green and red pastes into four jewels of each color. Attach to the crown using edible glue.

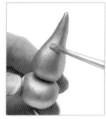

8 Make a paste with the gold luster powder and vodka, then paint the crown and the central detail with the resulting metallic paint. Leave to dry.

1 Roll out 3 oz. (90 g) of yellow paste and cut out the crown shape with the exacto knife. Once cut, immediately stand it up and coil it around. Join the ends using edible glue. Leave to dry.

Templates

On these pages, we feature line drawings for all the two-dimensional toppers in the book. Turn to page 82 to make your own template, or to learn how to scale these designs up or down.

Butterfly (page 108)

Swan (page 104)

Musical Notes (page 204)

Valentine Hearts (page 150)

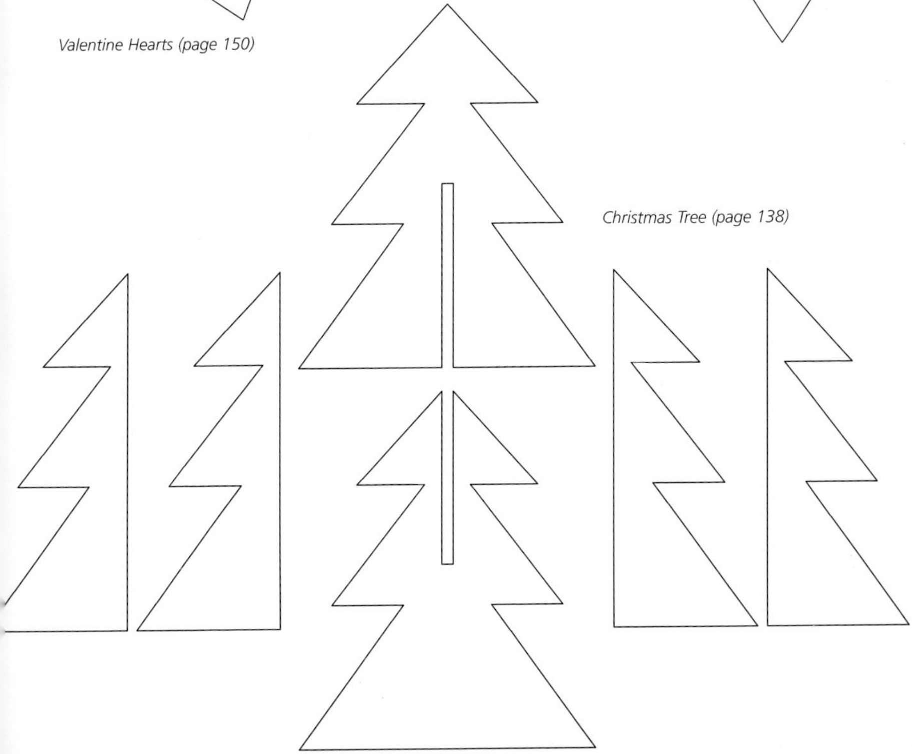

Christmas Tree (page 138)

index

A Note on Terminology

Cake decorating terminology can be confusing and difficult to grasp. As you begin to explore the world of fondant modeling, you will come to realize that many terms are used interchangeably—by beginners and experts alike. For clarity and consistency, we have used the following terminology in this book:

Fondant: the core ingredient in gum paste and flower paste; used as an umbrella term to describe gum paste, flower paste and rolled fondant.

Gum Paste: malleable, nonsticky medium used to make basic sugar shapes and nearly all the sugar models in this book.

Flower Paste: sometimes used as an alternative to gum paste, though not unlike it, flower paste is a soft and malleable paste that sets firmly when dry, making it good for delicate or detailed models.

Rolled Fondant: dough-like paste that is rolled out to cover cakes before they are decorated with fondant models.

credits

Author's acknowledgements

Thank you to Beverley and the team at Squires Kitchen for providing the modeling paste and food colors for cakes and models in this book. Squires Kitchen never fails to impress me with the quality of their products and the range that they are available in. Their staff is amazing, professional, friendly and helpful—and their distribution service is excellent and very reliable.

www.squires-shop.com
E: customer@squires-shop.com
T: 0845 61 71 810 (from UK)
T: +44 1252 260 260 (from outside UK)

I am very grateful to Kate and Chloe for guiding me through the making of this book, for being so supportive and for going above and beyond my expectations in assisting me with the practical details involved.